BIG HOOK **CROCHET**

35 projects to crochet using a **large** hook: hats, scarves, jewellery, baskets, rugs, cushions and more

Emma Friedlander-Collins

CICO BOOKS
LONDON NEW YORK

This book is dedicated to Monkey Collins – you rock.

Published in 2015 by CICO Books
An imprint of Ryland Peters & Small Ltd

20–21 Jockey's Fields   341 E 116th St
London WC1R 4BW   New York, NY 10029
www.rylandpeters.com

10 9 8 7 6 5 4 3 2 1

Text © Emma Friedlander-Collins 2015
Design, photography and illustration © CICO Books 2015

A CIP catalogue record for this book is available from the
Library of Congress and the British Library.

ISBN UK: 978 1 78249 250 4
ISBN US: 978 1 78249 251 1

Printed in China

Editor: Rachel Atkinson
Designer: Isobel Gillan
Photographer: Emma Mitchell
Stylist: Nel Haynes
Technique illustrators: Stephen Dew and Kate Simunek

Editor: Carmel Edmonds
In-house designer: Fahema Khanam
Art director: Sally Powell
Production controller: Sarah Kulasek-Boyd
Publishing manager: Penny Craig
Publisher: Cindy Richards

CONTENTS

INTRODUCTION

'Once upon a time there was a lady who had to spend a lot of time outdoors, day after day in the wind and the cold. The more layers she put on to keep warm, the tighter and tighter her winter coats became, until, after popping on a particularly cosy, chunky knit fisherman's sweater, she couldn't bend her arms at all. She refused to give up her beloved drummer boy jacket, and knew there *had* to be a more stylish answer to keep warm and toasty than a massive mountaineering coat.

She began a search for super chunky yarn, looking far and wide until, on a frosty day, she found some in the corner of a tiny craft shop. After buying the biggest hook they had, she ran all the way home and set to work. But, something was wrong. No matter what stitches she used, the yarn was so chunky and the hook so small, that her work always came out stiff and un-cuddly. Just when she thought all was lost and she'd have to give in and buy that massive mountaineering coat, her Beloved came to her rescue.

Using his magical engineering powers, he took her crochet hook, sawed the end off their kitchen broom, and set up a workbench in the dining room. Armed with a mighty saw, some squares of sandpaper, and his utterly mysterious grasp of maths, he hacked, sawed and sanded away, until, three hours later, having covered everything in the dining room in a layer of sawdust, he emerged with the most beautiful object the lady had ever seen; a lovingly crafted, perfectly up-scaled, 25mm crochet hook. She set to work instantly and the super-sized hook whipped through the super chunky yarn, making a soft, cuddly and sumptuous Super Snood.

The lady promised to use her super hook for the powers of good, and so this collection of patterns came to be.'

...and I hope you have as much fun making them as I did creating them. This collection of patterns is an homage to my Beloved and the beautiful super hook.

Emma Friedlander-Collins

BEFORE YOU BEGIN

Big hook crochet is a lot of fun and you can whip up wonderful projects in next to no time. Due to the size of the projects you will find that the way you hold the hook and yarn may be quite different to working on regular sized crochet projects, so follow these tips and tricks to get the most out of your new hobby.

TIPS & HINTS

- Some of the bigger projects in the book are remarkably heavy, but the speed at which they grow is so fast that you can whip projects up in no time at all. When working on larger projects, such as the rugs and baskets, you may find it easier to work on a table or the floor rather than your lap. Try crocheting around the project itself rather than turning it in circles when the weight becomes too much.
- Big hook crochet is a lot more physically demanding than ordinary crochet, so take regular breaks to flex and stretch your hands, arms and shoulders.

- It is worth noting that because of the size, fancier stitches can get a bit lost, and tend to look messy and confused; what big hook crochet really lends itself to is simplistic stitches, patterns in bold colours, statement pieces and sturdy homewares.

YARN

While looking for ways to make supersized crochet, I found a couple of yarns that are ideal just as they are; Cygnet 'Seriously Chunky' can be worked up on its own, as can Hoooked 'Zpagetti' or most recycled jersey yarns, but big hook crochet is also a perfect way to start using up the yarn stash! The Bedroll (page 58) was a way to just start ploughing through it all – 5 strands held together to make one supersized yarn, joining in new ones as the old ones ran out. Initially it can feel a little like taking a herd of cats for a walk, with all the strands from the different balls rolling around in different directions, but you'll soon get the hang of it!

- In many of the projects the thickness of the yarn, or yarn bundle, makes it difficult to tension the yarn in your usual way – experiment with holding the yarn until you find a solution that is comfortable and works best for you.
- Rather than buying three balls of yarn to work together, split one ball down into three smaller balls. Use a set of scales to work out how heavy each little ball should be.
- Jersey yarns can often vary in thickness, so it's worth unwinding a bit of each to determine how different colours vary – you may find you only need to work with one strand of one and two of another.
- Each pattern includes a 'How many strands?' section, telling you how to divide the yarn and how many ends you need to work the project with.

- You will find additional speciality yarns featuring in a few of the projects, details of which are given with each project.

EQUIPMENT

Crochet hooks: The main hook used in the book is size 25mm (US U/50) with a number of projects using a slightly smaller 23mm hook (sub for a 22mm hook if you can't find a 23mm hook), but you will need a few other sizes for various projects:

Crochet hooks used in the book:

25mm	US U/50
23mm	—
22mm	US T
9mm	US M/13
6mm	US J/10
5mm	US H/8
4mm	US G/6
2.75mm	US C/2

Tapestry & yarn needles: Tapestry needles just don't come big enough for a lot of the yarns used in the book! Use a smaller crochet hook in place of a needle for working in those fiddly ends or stitching things together, or search out a bodkin or split-eye needle. You may find that for some of the larger projects you can just use your fingers to weave pieces together!

Tape measure: Always handy for checking finished sizes.

SKILL LEVEL

Each project includes a star rating as a skill level guide and you will find the techniques you will need for each level listed below:

★☆☆ Projects for first-time crocheters using basic stitches with minimal shaping.

★★☆ Projects using yarn with basic stitches, repetitive stitch patterns, simple colour changes and simple shaping and finishing.

★★★ Projects using a variety of techniques, such as basic lace patterns or colour patterns, and mid-level shaping and finishing.

ABBREVIATIONS

BLO	Back loop only
BPtr	Back post treble crochet
cm	Centimetre(s)
ch	Chain
ch-sp	Chain-space
dc	Double crochet
dc2tog	Double crochet 2 stitches together
dtr	Double treble crochet
FLO	Front loop only
FPtr	Front post treble crochet
g	Gram(s)
htr	Half treble
htr2tog	Half treble crochet 2 stitches together
in	Inch(es)
LH	Left hand
m	Metre(s)
mm	Millimetre(s)
oz	Ounce(s)
rep	Repeat
RH	Right hand
RS	Right side of work
sl	Slip
sl st	Slip stitch
sp	Space
st(s)	Stitch(es)
tr	Treble crochet
tr2tog	Treble crochet 2 stitches together
yd(s)	Yard(s)
yrh	Yarn round hook
WS	Wrong side of work

chapter one

CLOTHES & ACCESSORIES

BOBBLE COWL

You know how sometimes you learn a new stitch and then want to use it on EVERYTHING? Well, this bobble stitch is one of those stitches! I love everything about it; from the technique for making it to the finished texture. Having used it in smaller projects, I then wondered what it would be like supersized and this brilliant cowl was born. In my head it hits 'uber fashionista statement cowl' levels and I see it slung over a tweed jacket with a flat cap. It is so warm – really cosy, snuggly and quick to make when the weather turns.

FOR THE COWL

Holding 2 strands of yarn A together, work 30ch, sl st in first ch to join taking care not to twist.

Round 1: Work Starting Bobble (see Pattern Notes) in first ch, miss next ch, *work Bobble (see Pattern Notes) in next ch, miss next ch; rep from * to end, sl st in top of Starting Bobble to join.

Round 2: Working into the top of bobbles from previous round, work Starting Bobble in first st, Bobble in each st to end, sl st in top of Starting Bobble to join.

Rounds 3–5: Rep Round 2.

Fasten off yarn A, and holding two strands together, join yarn B and work 1ch, (2dc) in each st around, sl st in first dc to join.

Fasten off.

Rejoin yarn B to opposite edge at the Starting Bobble, 1ch, (2dc) in the bottom of each bobble of Round 1, sl st in first dc to join.

Fasten off.

FINISHING

Weave in all loose ends and gently block to measurements.

PATTERN NOTES

The cowl uses two special stitches as detailed below:

- **Starting Bobble**: 3ch, work 4trtog into same stitch as follows: (yrh, insert hook into stitch, yrh, pull through stitch, yrh, pull through first two loops) four times into same stitch, yrh, pull through all five loops on hook. (1 loop remaining on hook)
- **Bobble**: Work 5trtog into same stitch as follows: (yrh, insert hook into stitch, yrh, pull through stitch, yrh, pull through first two loops) five times into same stitch, yrh, pull through all six loops on hook. (1 loop remaining on hook)

SKILL LEVEL

★★☆

SIZE

One size: 91cm (36in) circumference x 28cm (11in) deep

YOU WILL NEED

Yarn

Rowan, Big Wool (super chunky weight; 100% wool)

- 3 x 100g (3¾ oz) balls (80m / 87yds) in shade 064 Prize (**A**)
- 1 x 100g (3¾ oz) ball (80m / 87yds) in shade 025 Wild Berry (**B**)

How many strands?

Two strands are held together throughout.
Note: Split one of the colour **A** balls into two smaller and equal balls, and the colour **B** ball into two.

Hooks & Notions

25mm (US U/50) crochet hook
Large-eyed tapestry needle

TENSION

Tension is not critical but adjust the hook size to produce a flexible fabric.

ABBREVIATIONS

See page 9.

INFINITY SCARF

I love autumn. I mean, *I really love* autumn. I endure the awful, brash heat of summer knowing that soon the cooler weather and glorious autumn colours will appear, giving me the perfect excuse to dig out my woollen accessories and make more! I could probably have made a whole book just of giant scarves and cowls; in fact, I have a ridiculous number, most of them big and 'statementy', because when it's cool enough to wear a little blazer, or an oversized cardigan, nothing sets it off quite like a pop of chunky crochet.

SKILL LEVEL
 ★ ☆ ☆

SIZE
One size: 167cm (66in) circumference x 15cm (6in) deep

YOU WILL NEED
Yarn
Cygnet, Chunky (chunky weight; 100% acrylic)
- 9 x 100g (3½ oz) balls (156m / 170yds per ball) in shade 686 Gold

How many strands?
Work with nine strands held together.

Hooks & Notions
25mm (US U/50) crochet hook
6mm (US J/10) crochet hook for joining seams
Large-eyed tapestry needle

TENSION
Tension is not critical but adjust the hook size to produce a flexible fabric.

ABBREVIATIONS
See page 9.

FOR THE INFINITY SCARF
Holding one end from each ball of yarn (9 in total) and using the 25mm (US U/50) hook, make 8ch.
Row 1: 1tr in fourth ch from hook (missed 3 ch counts as first tr), 1tr in each st to end, turn. (6 sts)
Rows 2–33: 3ch (counts as first tr), miss first st, 1tr in each st to end, turn.
Fasten off.

FINISHING AND MAKING UP
Weave in all loose ends and gently block to measurements.

Using several strands of yarn held as one, whip stitch the two short ends of the scarf together. You may find it easier to do this using the 6mm (US J/10) crochet hook rather than a tapestry needle.

PATTERN NOTES
- The Infinity Scarf is easy to size up or down by adjusting the starting chain and number of rows.
- You will only need 500g (17½ oz) of yarn in total to make the scarf so if preferred you can work holding two ends from four balls and one end from a fifth, but please bear in mind it can get very tangled – honestly, it's easier to work from 9 separate balls!

AUTUMN COLOURS
This project is made in a beautiful shade of golden yellow as an homage to the turning autumn leaves, but you could substitute it for your own favourite leafy colour.

I-CORD NECKLACE

I've said it before, and I'll say it again, the crochet 'I-cord' used in this project is something I could happily make for hours! The same technique is used for the Bangle (page 26) and Christmas Wreath (page 55), but I am sure you could find a hundred other uses for it too. I chose an amazing orange yarn for a bright pop of colour, but use navy, steel grey or a neutral for a more pared-down look.

FOR THE NECKLACE

Holding two strands of yarn A with one strand of yarn B, work crochet I-cord for 25 rows as follows:

Step 1: Leaving a 30cm (12in) tail, make 3ch.

Step 2: Insert hook in second ch from hook, yrh and pull up a loop so you have 2 loops on the hook.

Step 3: Insert hook in third ch, yrh and pull up a loop so you have 3 loops on the hook.

Step 4: Carefully unhook the first 2 loops, and because this is big crochet, you can slip them over a finger to keep them safe or just hold them tightly, yrh and pull through the remaining loop on your hook leaving 1 loop on the hook.

Step 5: Place the next loop from your finger back on the hook, yrh and pull through this loop only. 2 loops now on the hook.

Step 6: Place the final loop from your finger back on your hook, yrh and pull through. 3 loops now on the hook.

Repeat Steps 4–6 **only** a further 24 times.

Work a sl st through all 3 loops to finish and fasten off leaving a second 30cm (12in) tail.

FINISHING

Do not weave the ends in but use these to tie the necklace in place at the back of your neck.

PATTERN NOTES

• The length and style of the necklace is easy to adjust and adapt – keep working I-cord to create a much longer necklace or one that will loop around several times.

• Change the gold metallic yarn for a fine mohair or novelty yarn to create a different look.

SKILL LEVEL

★ ☆ ☆

SIZE

One size: 102cm (40in) total length; 41cm (16in) length of I-cord, and 2 x 30cm (12in) tails for fastening

YOU WILL NEED

Yarn

Lion Brand, Hometown USA (super chunky weight; 100% acrylic)

• 1 x 142g (5 oz) ball (74m / 81yds per ball) in shade 401 Neon Orange (**A**)

Twilleys of Stamford, Goldfingering (4ply weight; 80% viscose, 20% metallic polyester)

• 1 x 25g (1 oz) ball (100m / 109yds per ball) in shade 0002 Gold (**B**)

How many strands?

Work with three strands held together; two of yarn **A** (one from each end of the ball) and one strand of yarn **B**.

Hooks & Notions

25mm (US U/50) crochet hook

TENSION

Tension is not critical but adjust the hook size to produce a flexible fabric.

ABBREVIATIONS

See page 9.

BICYCLE SADDLE & HANDLEBAR COVERS

This set was a request from my sister, starting with the saddle cover as a way to add cushiony comfort to the ride, with the handlebar covers making a natural accompaniment. As the weather starts to turn, any bike rider will tell you that the first things to feel the cold are your fingers, so pop these covers over the handlebars and you can warm your fingers in a flash!

SKILL LEVEL

SIZE
One size (adjustable to fit a range of bicycles):
- Saddle cover: 26cm (10in) across (at widest point) x 28cm (11in) long
- Handlebar covers: 18cm (7in) wide x 9cm (3½in) deep

YOU WILL NEED
Yarn
Cygnet, Seriously Chunky (super chunky weight; 100% acrylic)
- 2 x 100g (3½ oz) balls (48m / 52yds per ball) in shade 350 Russet

How many strands?
Work with two strands held together.

Hooks & Notions
23mm crochet hook

Large-eyed tapestry needle

3 x 75cm (30in) lengths of 1.5cm (⅝in) wide ribbon or jersey yarn such as Zpagetti for lacing the accessories in place

TENSION
Tension is not critical but adjust the hook size to produce a firm fabric.

ABBREVIATIONS
See page 9.

FOR THE SADDLE COVER
Holding two strands of yarn together, make a magic ring (see page 103).
Round 1: 1ch, 6dc into the ring, sl st in first dc to join. (6 sts)
Round 2: 1ch, 1dc in first st, 1dc in next st, 2ch, *1dc in each of next 2 sts, 2ch; rep from * to end, sl st in first dc to join.
Round 3: 1ch, 1dc in first st, 1dc in next st, (2dc, 2ch, 2dc) in next ch-sp, *1dc in next 2 sts, (2dc, 2ch, 2dc) in next ch-sp; rep from * to end, sl st in first dc to join.
Round 4: 1ch, 1dc in first st, 1dc in each of next 3 sts, (2dc, 2ch, 2dc) in next ch-sp, *miss next st, 1dc in each of next 5 sts, (2dc, 2ch, 2dc) in next ch-sp; rep from * to last 2 sts, miss 1 st, 1dc in last st, sl st in first dc to join.
Fasten off.
Working in rows continue as follows:
Row 1: Rejoin yarn in any corner ch-sp, work 1ch, 1dc in ch-sp, 1dc in each of next 9 sts, 1dc in ch-sp at end, turn. (11 sts)
Row 2: 1ch, 1dc in each st to end, turn.
Row 3: 1ch, dc2tog, 1dc in next 7 sts, dc2tog. (9 sts)
Fasten off.

pattern continued overleaf

PATTERN NOTES
- The saddle cover starts being worked in the round before changing to rows.
- If you can't find a 23mm hook use a 25mm (US U/50) hook and make 1 less chain at the start.

FINISHING

Weave in all loose ends and gently block to measurements.

Take the 75cm (30in) length of ribbon or yarn and weave in and out all the way around the edge of the cover, gently pulling it to gather. Fit it over your bicycle saddle and pull as tight as you can so it fits neatly in place. Tie to secure.

FOR THE HANDLEBAR COVERS
Panel A (make 2 alike):
Holding two strands of yarn together, make 6ch.
Row 1: 1dc in second ch from hook, 1dc in each of next 4ch, turn. (5 sts)
Rows 2–4: 1ch, 1dc in each st to end, turn.
Fasten off.

Panel B (make 2 alike):
Holding two strands of yarn together, make 7ch.
Row 1: 1dc in second ch from hook, 1dc in next 5ch, turn. (6 sts)
Rows 2–4: 1ch, 1dc in each st to end, turn.
Fasten off.

FINISHING

Weave in all loose ends and gently block to measurements.

Lay one Panel B on top of one Panel A and stitch the short sides together. Take the 75cm (30in) length of ribbon or yarn and loosely lace it up the long edges of the bottom piece. Place over the handlebars of your bicycle, pulling tightly to fit. Tie to secure and repeat for second cover.

BICYCLE BASKET

I fell off my bicycle recently and damaged the front basket beyond repair. Instead of buying a replacement I thought, 'Surely I can make one?' and spent ages looking for rope or twine that would be chunky enough, yet soft enough, to crochet with. As I was tidying up, I found the old dustsheets we use when decorating and had a light bulb moment! That evening my husband found me quietly cutting up his precious sheets into strips to use as yarn for making my new basket with.

TO MAKE THE YARN
Cut your cotton sheet into a continuous strip as follows:
Cut a 2.5cm (1in) strip along one side to 2.5cm (1in) from the top edge, stop, turn the sheet 90 degrees and cut a strip along the side to 2.5cm (1in) from the edge, then turn the sheet another 90 degrees. Repeat to the required quantity. I prepared a quarter of the sheet but only used a fraction of that for the final project.

FOR THE BASKET
Using the cotton sheet yarn and 25mm (US U/50) hook, make a magic ring (see page 103).
Round 1: Work 6dc into the ring, join with sl st in first dc. (6 sts)
Round 2: 1ch, 2dc in each st around, join with sl st in first dc. (12 sts)
Round 3: 1ch, *2dc in next st, 1dc in next st; rep from * around, join with sl st in first dc. (18 sts)
Round 4: 1ch, *2dc in next st, 1dc in each of next 2 sts; rep from * around, join with sl st in first dc. (24 sts)
Round 5: 1ch, 1dc in BLO of each st around for this round only, join with sl st in first dc.
Round 6: 1ch, 1dc in each st around, join with sl st in first dc.

pattern continued overleaf

PATTERN NOTES
• The turning chain for the flower is a shorter length than usual when working treble crochet. This is so the edge looks more 'natural' when the rose is rolled up.

SKILL LEVEL
★★☆

SIZE
One size: 28cm (11in) diameter at top x 20cm (8in) depth

YOU WILL NEED
Yarn
Heavy duty cotton twill sheet (or any cotton sheet) – see left
Robin, DK (DK weight; 100% acrylic)
• 1 x 25g (1 oz) ball (75m / 82yds per ball) in shade 049 Peach (**A**)
• 1 x 25g (1 oz) ball (75m / 82yds per ball) in shade 019 Apple (**B**)

How many strands?
Work with a single strand of each yarn.

Hooks & Notions
25mm (US U/50) crochet hook
4mm (US G/6) crochet hook
Large-eyed tapestry needle
Sewing needle and thread
2 pairs of 2.5cm (1in) D-rings
Scissors

TENSION
Tension is not critical but adjust the hook size to produce a firm fabric.

ABBREVIATIONS
See page 9.

Round 7: 1ch, 1dc in each of next 7 sts, 2dc in next st, 1dc in each of next 7 sts, 2dc in next st, 1dc in each of next 7 sts, 2dc in next st, join with sl st in first dc. (27 sts)
Rounds 8–13: 1ch, 1dc in each st around, join with sl st in first dc. Fasten off.

FOR THE STRAPS (make 2 alike)
Cut a 30cm (12in) length of cotton yarn and hand stitch a pair of the D-rings to one end.
Attach them to the basket by feeding one strip through the top row of crochet, then approximately four or five rows below (depending on your bike), and feed the end back and through the D-rings around the handle bars.

FOR THE ROSE (make 2 alike)
Holding a single strand of yarn A and using the 4mm (US G/6) hook, make 111ch.
Row 1: 1tr in third ch from hook, 2ch, 1tr in same ch, *miss 2 ch, (1tr, 2ch, 1tr) in next ch; rep from * to end, turn.
Row 2: 2ch, 1tr in first st, 1ch, 2tr in ch-sp, *(2tr, 1ch, 2tr) in next ch-sp; rep from * to end, turn.
Row 3: 2ch, 7tr in first ch-sp, *1dc in sp between the two sets of 2tr from previous row, 7tr in next ch-sp; rep from * to end.
Fasten off.
Roll the crocheted strip up into a rose shape and stitch through all the layers to secure. Fasten off leaving a long tail for stitching onto the basket and weave in any other loose ends.

FOR THE LEAF (make 3 alike)
Holding a single strand of yarn B and using the 4mm (US G/6) hook, make 14ch, sl st in second ch from hook, 1dc in next st, 1htr in next st, 1tr in next 2 sts, 1dtr in each of next 4 sts, 1tr in each of next 3 sts, 5htr in last st. Working along the opposite side of the foundation ch, 1tr in each of next 3 ch, 1tr in each of next 4 ch, 1tr in each of next 2 ch, 1htr in next ch, 1dc in next ch, sl st in next ch.

Fasten off leaving a long tail for stitching onto the basket and weave in any other loose ends.

FINISHING
Stitch the roses and and leaves to your basket.

ADDING EMBELLISHMENT
• Cut old denim jeans into strips as a great alternative to the cotton sheet yarn.
• Use odds and ends from your stash to crochet as many flowers and leaves as you like for decoration.

SPARKLY COLLAR

I LOVE this project! If it had been made in a thin yarn with a small hook it would be all dainty and a bit too pretty for my taste, but oversized, with just the merest hint of fluff and sparkle, and it's perfect. The collar is really quick and easy to make – whip a few up to match different outfits or as gifts for friends.

SKILL LEVEL

SIZE
One size: 56cm (22in) long x 9cm (3½in) deep

YOU WILL NEED
Yarn
Cygnet, Seriously Chunky (super chunky weight; 100% acrylic)
- 2 x 100g (3½ oz) balls (48m / 52yds per ball) in shade 288 Cream
Small amount of lightweight fluffy and/or sparkly yarn

How many strands?
Work with three strands held together; two strands of super chunky with one strand of fluffy yarn.

Hooks & Notions
23mm crochet hook

Large-eyed tapestry needle

2m (2yds) of 1.5cm (⅝in) wide cream ribbon

TENSION
Tension is not critical but adjust the hook size to produce a flexible fabric.

ABBREVIATIONS
See page 9.

FOR THE COLLAR
Holding two strands of the super chunky yarn together with one strand of fluffy yarn, make 25ch.
Row 1: 1dc in second ch from hook, 1dc in each st to end, turn. (24 sts)
Row 2: *3ch, miss 1 st, sl st in next st; rep from * to end.
Fasten off.

FINISHING
Weave in all loose ends and gently block to measurements.

Weave the ribbon in and out between the double crochet stitches and use it to fasten the collar around your neck in a pretty bow.

PATTERN NOTES
- If you can't find a 23mm hook use a 25mm (US U/50) hook and make 2 fewer chains at the start.

YARN VARIATIONS
- *Experiment using two different colours of the super chunky yarn for a tweedy effect.*
- *Play with other lightweight, textured and novelty yarns from your stash to hold with the super chunky yarn to create different looks.*

I-CORD BANGLE

This pattern uses the same crochet 'I-cord' as the Necklace on page 16 but alternates colours every row to give a lovely chevron effect. I have a friend who is the queen of chevrons and has them on everything, so henceforth this bangle shall be known as 'The Susannah'!

SKILL LEVEL

SIZE
One size: To fit 13–17cm (5–6½in) wrist circumference

YOU WILL NEED
Yarn
Boodles, Textile Yarn (super chunky weight; upcycled reclaimed fabric)
- 1 x 450g (16 oz) cone in shade Blue (**A**)
- 1 x 450g (16 oz) cone in shade Lime Green (**B**)

How many strands?
Work holding two strands of yarn **A** alternated with two strands of yarn **B**. Before starting, wind approximately 10m (11yds) of each colour off into separate balls.

Hooks & Notions
25mm (US U/50) crochet hook
Large-eyed tapestry needle

TENSION
Tension is not critical but adjust the hook size to produce a firm fabric.

ABBREVIATIONS
See page 9.

FOR THE BANGLE
Holding two strands of yarn A together, alternating colours as indicated, work crochet I-cord for 14 rows as follows:

Step 1: Using yarn A, make 3ch.
Step 2: Insert hook in second ch from hook, yrh and pull up a loop so you have 2 loops on the hook.
Step 3: Insert hook in third ch, yrh and pull up a loop so you have 3 loops on the hook.
Step 4: Carefully unhook the first 2 loops, and because this is big crochet, you can slip them over a finger to keep them safe or just hold them tightly, change to yarn B leaving A attached, work yrh and pull through the remaining loop on your hook leaving 1 loop on the hook.
Step 5: Place the next loop from your finger back on the hook, yrh and pull through this loop only so you have 2 loops on the hook.
Step 6: Place the final loop from your finger back on your hook, yrh and pull through. 3 loops now on the hook.
Step 7: Change to yarn A and repeat Steps 4–6.
Step 8: Change to yarn B and repeat Steps 4–6.
Repeat Steps 7–8 until you have worked a total of 14 rows.
Work a sl st through all 3 loops to finish and fasten off both yarns.

FINISHING
Tie the ends together and weave into the bangle.

CHANGING THE FINISHED SIZE
Adjust the finished circumference of the bangle by working fewer or more rows of the I-cord.

BED JACKET

This quick bolero project takes classic Granny Chic styling and turns it on its head using super-chunky yarn and a big hook. Wear it in a fabulously geek chic way, thrown over a prim little shirt with a pair of skinny jeans. I will continue referring to it as a bed jacket though – I love the idea of propping myself up in bed with a box of chocolates and a good book, with this around my shoulders!

SKILL LEVEL
★ ★ ★

SIZE
One size: 91cm (36in) wide (from cuff to cuff) x 41cm (16in) long (down centre back)

YOU WILL NEED
Yarn
Cygnet, Seriously Chunky (super chunky weight; 100% acrylic)
- 4 x 100g (3½ oz) balls (48m / 52yds per ball) in shade 319 Sage

How many strands?
Work with one strand of yarn.

Hooks & Notions
23mm crochet hook

Large-eyed tapestry needle

TENSION
Tension is not critical but adjust the hook size to produce a flexible fabric.

ABBREVIATIONS
See page 9.

FOR THE BED JACKET
Holding a single strand of yarn, make 59ch.

Row 1: Miss 6 ch (turning ch + 3 missed ch), (1tr, (1ch, 1tr) 4 times) in next ch, miss 3 ch, *1dc in next st, miss 3 ch, (1tr, (1ch, 1tr) 4 times) in next ch, miss 3 ch; rep from * to last ch, 1tr in last ch, turn.

Row 2: 6ch (turning ch + 3ch), *1dc in centre of cluster from previous row (so miss (1tr, 1ch) twice, and dc in next tr), 3ch, miss (1ch, 1tr) twice and 1tr in dc from previous row, 3ch; rep from * to last cluster, miss (1tr, 1ch) twice, and dc in next tr, 3ch, miss (1ch, 1tr) twice, 1tr in top of turning ch, turn.

Row 3: 3ch (turning ch), miss 3 ch, (1tr, (1ch, 1tr) 4 times) in dc from previous row, miss 3 ch, *1dc in next tr from previous row, miss 3 ch, (1tr, (1ch, 1tr) 4 times) in next dc from previous row, miss 3 ch; rep from * to end, 1tr in top of turning ch, turn.

Rows 4–12: Work Rows 2 and 3 a further 4 times, then work Row 2 only once more.
Fasten off.

FINISHING
Weave in all loose ends and gently block to measurements.

Lay the rectangle flat with the long edges at top and bottom. Bring the bottom and top right-hand corners together, and join them by stitching a 25cm (10in) seam, working inwards from the outer edge. Repeat for the left-hand side.

PATTERN NOTES
- I find some stitches can get a bit lost when using the larger hooks, but this one, which is called 'open scallop', works well when it comes to subversive Granny Chic.
- To make a slightly larger bolero, use a 25mm (US U/50) hook, and purchase 1 more ball of yarn to ensure you have enough.

CHUNKY CUFF

I have a collection of sweat bands and wrist cuffs leftover from my more rock 'n' roll days but feel a little too grown-up to wear them now. Whilst doodling with some jersey yarn for the Necklace (page 16) and Bangle (page 26), I had an idea – how about a slightly softer and more decorative cuff so I can keep the rock 'n' roll vibe but in a way more befitting a grown-up lady!

FOR THE CUFF
Holding two strands of yarn A together, work 9ch.
Row 1: 1dc in second ch from hook, 1dc in each ch to end, turn. (8 sts)
Row 2: 1ch, 1dc in each st to end.
Fasten off leaving a 12in (30cm) tail.

FINISHING
Using the long tail, stitch the short edges of the cuff together. Weave in ends.

FOR THE EMBELLISHMENT
Using one of the contrasting strips, make a loop and push it through a crochet space in the middle of the cuff from back to front. Using the second contrast strip, and working into the space above the first, pass the end from back to front, through the loop of the first colour, and into the space below. Repeat this all along the cuff. Fasten off, tie the ends together and weave into the cuff.

COLOUR COMBINATIONS
There are so many options for customising this project – set a neutral or bright palette and experiment with different ribbons and trims for the contrast pattern to create different looks.

SKILL LEVEL
★ ☆ ☆

SIZE
One size: To fit 13–17cm (5–6½in) wrist circumference

YOU WILL NEED
Yarn
Boodles, Textile Yarn (super chunky weight; upcycled reclaimed fabric)
• 1 x 450g (16 oz) cone in shade Soft Red (A)
2 different, contrasting 50cm (20in) lengths of ribbon or jersey yarn

How many strands?
Two strands of yarn A held together. Before starting, wind approximately 10m (11yds) off into a separate ball.

Hooks & Notions
25mm (US U/50) crochet hook
Large-eyed tapestry needle

TENSION
Tension is not critical but adjust the hook size to produce a firm yet flexible fabric.

ABBREVIATIONS
See page 9.

MARKET BAG

I often pick up unplanned groceries and while I really dislike using plastic bags, making a reusable grocery bag out of wool just wasn't an option. The Hoooked Zpagetti recycled jersey yarn turned out to be the perfect answer! It can be worked on a smaller hook, but is used here with a larger one, which creates a lovely open weave, and the stretch in the yarn also means you can pack the bag really full.

SKILL LEVEL

★★☆

SIZE
One size: main bag: 25cm (10in) wide x 33cm (13in) deep; handle drop: 8cm (3in)

YOU WILL NEED
Yarn
Hoooked, Zpagetti (super chunky weight; 95% cotton, 5% elastane)
- 1 x 850g (30 oz) cone (120m / 131yds per cone) in shade Ibiza Sun

How many strands?
Work with one strand of yarn.

Hooks & Notions
25mm (US U/50) crochet hook
Large-eyed tapestry needle

TENSION
Tension is not critical but adjust the hook size to produce a flexible fabric.

ABBREVIATIONS
See page 9.

FOR THE BAG
Holding a single strand of yarn, make 15ch.
Round 1: 3dc in 2nd ch from hook, 1dc in each of next 12ch, 3dc in last ch, working back down the other side of the ch, 1dc in each of next 12ch, sl st in first dc to join. (30 sts)
Round 2: 3ch (counts as first tr), miss first st, 1tr in each st around, sl st in third ch of 3ch to join.
Round 3: 4ch (counts as first tr and 1ch), miss 2 sts, 1tr in next st, 1ch, miss 1 st, *1tr in next st, 1ch, miss 1 st; rep from * to end, sl st in third ch of 4ch to join.
Rounds 4–9: Rep Round 3.
Round 10: 3ch (counts as first tr), miss first st, 1tr in each st around, sl st in third ch of 3ch to join.
Continue as follows to form the handles:
Round 11: 1ch, 1dc in each of next 7 sts, 8ch, miss 5 sts, 1dc in each of next 9 sts, 8ch, miss 5 sts, 1dc in each of last 4 sts, sl st in first dc to join.
Round 12: 1ch, 1dc in each of next 7 sts, work 8dc around the 8ch from previous round, 1dc in each of next 9 sts, work 8dc around the 8ch from previous round, 1dc in each of last 4 sts, sl st in first dc to join. Fasten off.

FINISHING
Weave in all loose ends and gently block to measurements.

**HOMEMADE
JERSEY YARN**
*If you are feeling
adventurous, try making your
own jersey yarn from old
T-shirts. Search online
for tutorials.*

BOWLER HAT

I was only very young in the 1980s but that didn't stop me from wanting a ridiculously cool bowler hat just like the pop stars were wearing! When I spotted this insanely bright yarn, it screamed 1980s at me, and I knew exactly what it wanted to be; it wanted to be an homage to the cool kids of the 'Pretty in Pink' and 'Breakfast Club' era and I finally got the bowler hat of my dreams.

SKILL LEVEL
★★☆

SIZE
One size: To fit 56–61cm (22–24in) head circumference

YOU WILL NEED
Yarn
Wool and the Gang, Crazy Sexy Wool, (super chunky weight; 100% Peruvian wool)
- 1 x 200g (7 oz) ball (80m / 87yds per ball) in shade Fireball Orange (**A**)
- 1 x 200g (7 oz) ball (80m / 87yds per ball) in shade Candy Red (**B**)

How many strands?
Work with two strands held together.

Hooks & Notions
25mm (US U/50) crochet hook

Large-eyed tapestry needle

TENSION
Tension is not critical but adjust the hook size to produce a firm yet flexible fabric.

ABBREVIATIONS
See page 9.

FOR THE HAT
Holding both ends of yarn A together (1 from each end of the ball), make a magic ring (see page 103).

Round 1: Work 6dc into the ring, sl st in first dc to join. (6 sts)

Round 2: 1ch, 2dc in each st around, sl st in first dc to join. (12 sts)

Round 3: 3ch (counts as first tr), 1tr in first st, *1tr in next st, 2tr in next st; rep from * a further 4 times, 1tr in next st, sl st in third ch of 3ch to join. (18 sts)

Round 4: 3ch (counts as first tr), miss first st, 1tr in each st around, sl st in third ch of 3ch to join.

Break yarn A. Holding both ends of yarn B together (1 from each end of the ball), join yarn B and continue as follows for the brim:

Round 5: 3ch (counts as first tr), miss first st, 1tr in each st around, sl st in third ch of 3ch to join.

Rounds 6–7: Work Round 5 twice more.

Fasten off.

FINISHING
Weave in all loose ends and gently block to measurements.

Roll up the brim to give your hat a bowler style finish and secure with a few stitches.

PATTERN NOTES
- The hat is worked from the top downwards.

SUBTLER SHADES
For a more toned-down but equally fun bowler hat, choose a neutral shade or one that will work with your winter coat.

HOUSE BOOTS

There are so many reasons why you should make these amazing House Boots! They are super warm and cosy, and take only a couple of hours and just three balls of yarn to make. You can add as many pompoms as you like, and they are brilliant gifts for friends and family alike. What's not to love?!

SKILL LEVEL
★★☆

SIZE
One size: To fit ladies UK shoe size 5½–6½

YOU WILL NEED
Yarn
Red Heart, Lisa Big (super chunky; 100% acrylic)
- 1 x 200g (7 oz) balls (120m / 131yds per ball) in shade (136) Pink (**A**)
- 2 x 200g (7 oz) balls (120m / 131yds per ball) in shade (102) Nature (**B**)

How many strands?
Work with two strands of yarn held together throughout.

Hooks & Notions
25mm (US U/50) crochet hook
Large-eyed tapestry needle

TENSION
Tension is not critical but adjust the hook size to produce a firm yet flexible fabric.

ABBREVIATIONS
See page 9.

FOR THE BOOT UPPER (make 2 alike)
Holding 2 strands of yarn A together, make 16ch, join with a sl st in first ch.
Fasten off yarn A and holding two strands together, join yarn B.
Round 1: 1ch, 1dc in second ch from hook, 1dc in each ch around, sl st in first dc to join. (16 sts)
Rounds 2–6: 1ch, 1dc in each st around, sl st in first dc to join.
Fasten off yarn B and join yarn A.
Round 7: 1ch, 1dc in each st around, sl st in first dc to join.
Fasten off yarn A and join yarn B.
Round 8: 1ch, 1dc in each of next 2 sts, 2dc in each of next 3 sts, 1dc in each of next 11 sts, sl st in first dc to join. (19 sts)
Round 9: 1ch, 1dc in each of next 3 sts, 2dc in each of next 4 sts, 1dc in each of next 12 sts, sl st in first dc to join. (23 sts)
Round 10: 1ch, 1dc in each of next 5 sts, 2dc in each of next 4 sts, 1dc in each of next 14 sts, sl st in first dc to join. (27 sts)
Round 11: 1ch, 1dc in each of next 7 sts, 2 dc in each of next 3 sts, 1dc in each of next 17 sts, sl st in first dc to join. (30 sts)
Fasten off yarn B and join yarn A.
Round 12: 1ch, 1dc in each st around, sl st in first dc to join.
Fasten off.

FOR THE SOLE (make 2 alike)
Holding 2 strands of yarn A together, make 4ch.
Row 1: 1dc in second ch from hook, 1dc in each of next 2 ch, turn. (3 sts)
Rows 2–6: 1ch, 1dc in each st to end, turn.
Row 7: 1ch, 2dc in first st, 1dc in each of next 2 sts, turn.
Row 8: 1ch, 1dc in each st to end, turn.
Row 9: 1dc in first st, 1dc in each of next 2 sts, sl st in last st.
Fasten off.

FINISHING

Weave in all loose ends and gently block the separate pieces.

Stitch the soles to the upper working through the back loops only of the upper. Cut a length of yarn A and weave through the yarn A row in the middle of the boot – this acts as a drawstring around the ankle. If you happen to love pompoms as much as me, then make a couple to attach at the top.

TO POMPOM OR NOT TO POMPOM
It is up to you! The pompoms really do finish the boot off though, and you can go all out with leftovers from your stash to create co-ordinating or clashing ones for your boots.

NECK WARMER

My favourite yarn of all time is an enormous ball of unspun, roving yarn I picked up at a craft fair. It is very delicate to crochet with, but incredibly soft and smells delightfully 'sheepy' – you just want to sink right into it which makes it ideal for a squishy neckwarmer!

FOR THE NECK WARMER
Holding a single strand of roving, make 31ch.
Row 1: 1dc in second ch from hook, 1dc in each ch to end, turn. (30 sts)
Rows 2–7: 1ch, 1dc in each st to end.
Fasten off.

FINISHING
Weave in all loose ends and, very gently, steam block to even out the stitches.

Stitch both buttons to one end and use the natural weave of the crochet as buttonholes.

PATTERN NOTES
• This is a super-simple make but the delicate nature of the roving yarn means you must work gently. Take your time and don't pull the yarn – unwind more from the ball to prevent it breaking.

WASHING ROVING FIBRE
Roving fibre is generally used for spinning or felting, which makes laundering quite tricky. Look for machine washable roving blended with nylon to prevent your project becoming felted.

SKILL LEVEL
★★☆

SIZE
One size: 99cm (39in) wide x 23cm (9in) deep, unbuttoned and laid flat

YOU WILL NEED
Yarn
Approximately 500g (17½ oz) of roving fibre in a natural shade

How many strands?
Work with one strand of the roving.

Hooks & Notions
25mm (US U/50) crochet hook
2 x 5cm (2in) large buttons
Large-eyed tapestry needle

TENSION
Tension is not critical but adjust the hook size to produce a flexible fabric.

ABBREVIATIONS
See page 9.

GRANNY CHIC SLIPPERS

There is a lot of Granny Chic throughout this collection of patterns and these slippers are no exception! I thought really hard about making a sling-back, moccasin or harem style slipper, but when it got right down to it, what I really, *really* wanted was something to make me feel cuddled when returning home following a damp and chilly walk. Forget elegance, forget dainty, go granny!

SKILL LEVEL

★★☆

SIZE

S (M, L); to fit ladies UK shoe size: 3–4 (5–6, 7–8)

YOU WILL NEED

Yarn

Cygnet, Seriously Chunky (super chunky weight; 100% acrylic)

- 1 x 100g (3½ oz) balls (48m / 52yds per ball) in shade 4884 Barley (**A**)
- 1 x 100g (3½ oz) balls (48m / 52yds per ball) in shade 288 Cream (**B**)

Hoooked, Zpagetti (super chunky weight; 95% cotton, 5% elastane)

- 1 x 850g (30 oz) cone (120m / 131yds per cone) in shade Ibiza Sun (**C**)

How many strands?

Work with two strands held together for the sole: one each of yarn **A** and **C**.

Work with one strand of yarn **B** for the shoe upper.

Hooks & Notions

25mm (US U/50) crochet hook

Large-eyed tapestry needle

TENSION

Tension is not critical but adjust the hook size to produce a firm fabric.

ABBREVIATIONS

See page 9.

FOR THE SLIPPER (make 2 alike)

Holding yarns A and C together, make 8 (10, 12) ch.

Round 1: 2dc in second ch from hook, 1dc in each of next 5 (6, 7) ch, 3dc in last ch, then working back along the other side of foundation ch, work 1dc in each of next 5 (6, 7) ch, 1dc in end ch, sl st in first dc to join. (16 (18, 20) sts)

Round 2: 1ch, 2dc in first st, 1dc in each of next 7 (8, 9) sts, 2dc in next st, 1dc in each of next 7 (8, 9) sts, sl st in first dc to join. (18 (20, 22) sts)
Fasten off yarns A and C.

Join a single strand of yarn B and continue as follows:

Round 3: 1ch, working in BLO for this round only, 1dc in each st to end, sl st in first dc to join.

Round 4: 1ch, 1dc in each of next 6 (7, 8) sts, (dc2tog) 3 times, 1dc in each of next 6 (7, 8) sts, sl st in first dc to join. (15 (17, 19) sts)

Round 5: 1ch, 1dc in each of next 7 (8, 9) sts, dc2tog, 1dc in each of next 6 (7, 8) sts, sl st in first dc to join. (14 (16, 18) sts)
Fasten off.

FINISHING

Weave in all loose ends and gently block to measurements.

Take a length of the Zpagetti yarn, thread it through the last round worked and tie in a bow at the front.

PATTERN NOTES

- The soles are made using one strand each of yarns A and C held together to give the slipper added durability.
- Where only one number is given this applies to all sizes.

FINISHING TOUCHES

Dig a length of ribbon, fabric or decorative trim out of your craft supplies to use in place of the Zpagetti tie around the top of each slipper – I love the idea of a big oversized bow on these!

COWBOY KERCHIEF

I have a lot of cowls and scarves but I find most of them are too big to wear indoors and wanted something that I could throw on over a T-shirt for wearing around the house and office. This mini shawl is perfect! Wear it kerchief style around your neck to keep winter and air conditioning chills off your neck.

SKILL LEVEL

SIZE
One size: 170cm (67in) wide x 45cm (18in) deep

YOU WILL NEED
Yarn
Lion Brand, Hometown USA (super chunky weight; 100% acrylic)
- 1 x 142g (5 oz) ball (74m / 81yds) per ball) in shade 149 Dallas Grey (**A**)
- 1 x 142g (5 oz) ball (74m / 81yds) per ball) in shade 100 New York White (**B**)

How many strands?
Work with a single strand of each yarn.

Hooks & Notions
25mm (US U/50) crochet hook
Large-eyed tapestry needle

TENSION
Tension is not critical but adjust the hook size to produce a flexible fabric.

ABBREVIATIONS
See page 9.

FOR THE KERCHIEF
Holding a single strand of yarn A, make 4ch.
Row 1: 2tr in fourth ch from hook, turn. (1 3tr cluster made – first 3ch is the turning ch and counts as tr here and throughout)
Fasten off yarn A and join yarn B.
Row 2: 3ch (counts as 1tr), 2tr in first st, 1ch, miss 1 st, 3tr in last st, turn.
Fasten off yarn B and rejoin yarn A.
Row 3: 3ch (counts as 1tr), 2tr in first st, 1ch, 3tr in next ch-sp, 1ch, miss 2 sts, 3tr in last st, turn.
Fasten off yarn A and rejoin yarn B.
Row 4: 3ch (counts as 1tr), 2tr in first st, *1ch, 3tr in next ch-sp; rep from * to last 3tr cluster, 1ch, miss 2 sts, 3tr in last st, turn.
Rows 5–10: Repeat Row 4, continuing to alternate yarns A and B as set.
After Row 10, do not fasten off yarn B, but continue as follows:
Row 11: 10ch, 1dc in second ch from hook, 1dc in each of next 8 ch, work 1dc in each tr of the scarf, 10ch, turn, 1dc in second ch from hook, 1dc in each of next 8 ch, sl st into body of scarf.
Fasten off.

FINISHING
Weave in all loose ends and gently block to measurements.

Add pompoms if desired.

POMPOM FUN
If you have a pompom fixation like me, this kerchief looks adorable with one on each end of the ties!

SUPER SNOOD

This was my very first big hook crochet project! I had the yarn and idea for a snood and set to work with my size 16mm hook, but the finish was much stiffer than I wanted. So my Beloved worked his engineering magic and made the most beautiful big crochet hook ever! The snood then crocheted up exactly as I had imagined it, soft and smooshy, and with the addition of the body warmer it has become a vital piece of winter clothing.

SKILL LEVEL

SIZE
One size:
- Snood section: 46cm (18in) deep, 81cm (32in) circumference
- Body warmer section (measured flat): 48cm (19in) long, 33cm (13in) wide at bust point, 46cm (18in) wide at hip

YOU WILL NEED
Yarn
Cygnet, Seriously Chunky (super chunky weight; 100% acrylic)
- 7 x 100g (3½ oz) balls (48m / 52yds per ball) in shade 288 Cream

How many strands?
Work with one strand of yarn.

Hooks & Notions
25mm (US U/50) crochet hook

6mm (US J/10) crochet hook for joining seams

Large-eyed tapestry needle

TENSION
Tension is not critical but adjust the hook size to produce a flexible fabric.

ABBREVIATIONS
See page 9.

FOR THE SNOOD
Holding a single strand of yarn and using the 25mm (US U/50) hook, make 30ch, join with a sl st to make a circle taking care not to twist.
Round 1: 1ch, 1dc in each ch around, sl st in first dc to join. (30 sts)
Rounds 2–26: 1ch, 1dc in each st, sl st in first dc to join.
Fasten off leaving a long tail for seaming.

FOR THE FRONT AND BACK PANELS (make 2 alike)
Holding a single strand of yarn and using the 25mm (US U/50) hook, make 17ch.
Row 1: 1dc in second ch from hook, 1dc in each ch to end, turn. (16 sts)
Rows 2–16: 1ch, 1dc in each st to end, turn.
Fasten off leaving a long tail for seaming.

pattern continued overleaf

PATTERN NOTES
- The Super Snood is made in four separate pieces which are then joined together.
- The size is easy to adjust to fit you by making the starting chain for the bottom piece long enough to go around your hips. Once this measurement is set the rest will fit.
- The turning chain counts as a stitch throughout.

FOR THE BOTTOM PANEL

Using the 25mm (US U/50) hook, make 38ch, join with a sl st to make a circle taking care not to twist.

Rows 1–4: 1ch, 1dc in each st, sl st in first ch to join. (38 sts)

Fasten off leaving a long tail for seaming.

FINISHING

Lay the short edge of the front panel so that it sits along the centre of the front edge of the snood, and seam together using the 6mm (US J/10) hook or a tapestry needle and a length of yarn.

Place the short edge of the back panel along the same edge but on the opposite side of the snood and seam together. There should be 2–3 sts of snood on either side between the front and back panels.

Place the bottom panel so the top edge meets the bottom of the front panel and stitch in place, then repeat for the back panel.

Weave in all loose ends and gently block to measurements.

BOLD PANELS

Work the snood and body warmer sections in contrasting colours for a modern colour-block look.

CLOCHE HAT

This hat was born out of my obsession with *The Hunger Games* and the bird was designed to look like a Mockingjay, but my husband disagrees! Either way it's a cute take on the 1920s cloche hats, upsized and updated for big hooks and chunky yarn.

FOR THE HAT
Holding 6 strands of yarn A together, and using the 23mm crochet hook, make a magic ring (see page 103).
Round 1: 1ch, work 6dc into the ring, sl st in first dc to join. (6 sts)
Round 2: 1ch, 2dc in each st around, sl st in first dc to join. (12 sts)
Round 3: 1ch, *2dc in first st, 1dc in next st; rep from * to end, sl st in first dc to join. (18 sts)
Round 4: 1ch, *2dc in first st, 1dc in each of next 2 sts; rep from * to end, sl st in first dc to join. (24 sts)
Rounds 5–9: 1ch, 1dc in each st around, sl st in first dc to join. (24 sts)
Round 10: 1ch, *1dc in each of next 5 sts, 2dc in next st; rep from * to end, sl st in first dc to join. (28 sts)
Round 11: 1ch, *1dc in each of next 6 sts, 2dc in next st; rep from * to end, sl st in first dc to join. (32 sts)
Fasten off.

FOR THE BIRD MOTIF HEAD
Holding a single strand of yarn B, and using the 2.75mm (US C/2) hook, make 3ch, join with sl st in first ch.
Round 1: 3ch (counts as first tr), 5tr into ring, join with a sl st in 3ch, work 3ch and sl st back into sl st to make the beak.

pattern continued overleaf

PATTERN NOTES
- The bird motif is made in four pieces, then stitched together.
- You will only need 200g (7 oz) of yarn A in total to make the hat, so if preferred you can work from two balls of yarn and wind them into six equal balls.

SKILL LEVEL

SIZE
One size. To fit: 56–61cm (22–24in) head circumference

Bird motif: 6cm (2½in) across

YOU WILL NEED
Yarn
Red Heart, Shimmer (DK weight; 97% acrylic, 3% polyester)
- 6 x 100g (3½ oz) balls (256m / 280yds per ball) in shade 07 Lime (**A**)

Twilleys of Stamford, Goldfingering (4ply weight; 80% viscose, 20% polyester)
- 1 x 25g (1 oz) ball (100m / 109yds per ball) in shade 02 Gold (**B**)

How many strands?
Work with six strands of yarn **A** held together for the hat.

Work with a single strand of yarn **B** for the bird motif.

Hooks & Notions
23mm crochet hook

2.75mm (US C/2) crochet hook

Large-eyed tapestry needle

TENSION
Tension is not critical but adjust the hook size to produce a flexible fabric.

ABBREVIATIONS
See page 9.

FOR THE BIRD MOTIF BODY

Holding a single strand of yarn B, and using the 2.75mm (US C/2) hook, make 4ch.

Row 1: 1dc in second ch from hook, 1dc in each of next 2 sts, turn. (3 sts)

Row 2: 1ch, 1dc in each st to end, turn.

Row 3: 1ch, 1dc in each of next 2 sts, 2dc in next st, turn. (4 sts)

Row 4: 1ch, 1dc in each st to end, turn.

Row 5: 1ch, dc2tog, 1dc in each of next 2 sts, turn. (3 sts)

Row 6: 1ch, 1dc in each st to end, turn.

Row 7: 1ch, 1dc in each st to end, turn.

Row 8: 5ch, sl st in second ch from hook, sl st in next ch, 1dc in next 2 ch, sl st back into the body.

Row 9: Repeat Row 8.

Fasten off.

FOR THE BIRD MOTIF WINGS (make 2 alike)

Holding a single strand of yarn B, and using the 2.75mm (US C/2) hook, make 12ch.

Row 1: Sl st in second ch from hook, sl st in each of next 2 ch, 1dc in each of next 3 ch, 1tr in each of next 2 ch, 3tr in next ch, 1tr in each of next 2 ch.

Fasten off.

FINISHING

For the hat, weave in all loose ends and gently block to measurements.

Tack up one side of the brim with a few stitches.

Join the four sections of the bird motif together. Weave in all loose ends, gently block to measurements and stitch in place on the upturned brim of the hat.

BIRD DECORATION
Use any fine contrasting yarn to create the bird – in fact, why stop at one? You could make a whole flock!

chapter two
HOMEWARE

BASKET WEAVE CUSHION

This was one of those stitches I had been obsessing about trying in a project for some time. When worked on a small hook with lightweight yarn it has a lovely textured finish, but I couldn't find quite the right use for it. Then I spotted a beautiful soft grey throw with a blanket stitch edging in a magazine and everything just came together.

SKILL LEVEL

SIZE
One size: 40cm (16in) square

YOU WILL NEED

Yarn
Cygnet, Chunky (chunky weight; 100% acrylic)
- 8 x 100g (3½ oz) balls (155m / 170yds per ball) in shade 195 Light Grey (**A**)
- 5 x 100g (3½ oz) balls (155m / 170yds per ball) in shade 686 Gold (**B**)

How many strands?
Work with eight strands of yarn **A** held together and five strands of yarn **B** held together.

Hooks & Notions
23mm crochet hook
Large-eyed tapestry needle
40cm (16in) square cushion insert

TENSION
Tension is not critical but adjust the hook size to produce a firm yet flexible fabric.

ABBREVIATIONS
See page 9.

FOR THE CUSHION COVER (make 2 alike)
Holding 8 strands of yarn A together (1 from each ball), make 18ch.
Row 1: 1tr in third ch from hook, 1tr in each ch to end, turn. (16 sts)
Row 2: 3ch, *1FPtr around each of next 3 sts, 1BPtr around each of next 3 sts; rep from * once more, 1FPtr around each of next 3 sts, 1tr in last st, turn.
Row 3: 3ch, 1tr in first st, *1FPtr around each of next 3 sts, 1BPtr around each of next 3 sts; rep from * once more, 1FPtr around each of next 3 sts, turn.
Rows 4–12: Repeat Rows 2 and 3 a further 4 times then Row 2 once more.
Fasten off.

pattern continued overleaf

PATTERN NOTES
- Starting chain does not count as a stitch.
- If preferred you can work from three balls of yarn B, holding both ends from two balls (one from each end) and one end from the third, but please bear in mind it can get very tangled and it's much easier to work from 5 separate balls!
- If you can't find a 23mm hook use a 25mm (US U/50) hook and make 1 less chain at the start, then omit the final 1tr of Row 2/first 1tr of Row 3.

FINISHING

Weave in all loose ends and gently block to measurements.

Holding the two panels together, and working with 5 strands of yarn B held together, join the yarn at one corner working through both panels here and throughout. Work 1ch, 3dc in same corner st, 1dc through each of next 13 sts, 3dc in corner st, 1dc around each of the 12 row ends, 3dc in corner st. Stuff the cover with the cushion insert, then work 1dc in each st along the bottom edge, 3dc in corner st and 1dc around each of the 12 row ends along the last edge, join with a slip stitch in first dc.

Fasten off and weave in any remaining loose ends.

A NEW LOOK

New cushions are a great way to freshen the look of a room. Work in a shade to blend with your decor, or go bright and contrast with a pop of colour.

CHRISTMAS WREATH

The magic of crochet 'I-cord' appears again in this beautiful Christmas Wreath. When combined with my second favourite tool in my craft room, the pompom maker (the first is of course my crochet hook), I am filled with joy! The pictured wreath is made in a tasteful winter palette, but would look amazing in classic red and green—or how about an orange and black version for Halloween, or multi-coloured for parties?

FOR THE WREATH

Holding a strand from each ball of yarn together (8 in total), work crochet I-cord for 30 rows as follows:

Step 1: Leaving a 30cm (12in) tail, make 3ch.

Step 2: Insert hook in second ch from hook, yrh and pull up a loop so you have 2 loops on the hook.

Step 3: Insert hook in third ch, yrh and pull up a loop so you have 3 loops on the hook.

pattern continued overleaf

SIZE
One size: 23cm (9in) diameter

YOU WILL NEED
Yarn

Sirdar, Big Softie (super chunky weight; 51% wool, 49% acrylic)
- 2 x 50g (1¾ oz) balls (45m / 49yds per ball) in shade 335 Blancmange

King Cole, Glitz (DK weight; 100% acrylic)
- 2 x 100g (3½) balls (290m / 317yds per ball) in shade 483 Diamond White

Twilleys of Stamford, Goldfingering (4ply weight; 80% viscose, 20% polyester)
- 1 x 25g (1 oz) ball (100m / 109yds per ball) in shade 010 White

Boodles, Textile Yarn (super chunky weight; upcycled reclaimed fabric)
- 1 x 450g (16 oz) cone in shade White

Robin, DK (DK weight; 100% acrylic)
- 1 x 25g (1 oz) ball (75m / 82yds per ball) in shade 278 Sky Blue
- 1 x 25g (1 oz) ball (75m / 82yds per ball) in shade 070 White

How many strands?

Work with eight strands held together, one from each individual ball of yarn.

Hooks & Notions
25mm (US U/50) crochet hook

Large-eyed tapestry needle

Pompom maker or card

Craft wire

TENSION
Tension is not critical but adjust the hook size to produce a firm fabric.

ABBREVIATIONS
See page 9.

Step 4: Carefully unhook the first 2 loops, and because this is big crochet, you can slip them over a finger to keep them safe or just hold them tightly, yrh and pull through the remaining loop on your hook leaving 1 loop on the hook.

Step 5: Place the next loop from your finger back on the hook, yrh and pull through this loop only so you have 2 loops on the hook.

Step 6: Place the final loop from your finger back on your hook, yrh and pull through. 3 loops now on the hook.

Repeat Steps 4–6 **only** a further 29 times.

Work a sl st through all 3 loops to finish and fasten off leaving a second 30cm (12in) tail.

FINISHING

Tie the tail ends together and leave as a bow or weave into the wreath.

Weave the craft wire through the back of the i-cord to help hold its shape, taking care to twist the ends together and tuck inside the wreath safely out of the way.

Make as many or as few pompoms as you like and attach to the wreath. I placed mine across the join of the i-cord, then added tree decorations for a little extra festiveness.

USING UP LEFTOVERS
• *Make more pompoms from the leftovers and use them as tags when gift wrapping.*
• *Pompoms can be made from any yarn, so raid your yarn stash for any part-balls or novelty yarns that would suit the project.*

CAMPING ROLL

This roll is great to take camping, too! Instead of spending a night on an air mattress and ending up cold and achy all over, simply take this with you to add an extra layer of padding and warmth.

BEDROLL & BENCH COVER

This was my first experiment with crocheting lots of yarns together. I went through the stash, picked out colours that I had the most of and got to work with the big crochet hook. The idea was to make a comfy bedroll that I could take outside for lounging in the garden, but I found that it worked as extra padding on any bench or bed. The finished project is slightly longer than a standard bedroll, so you can roll one end up to use as a built-in cushion – or if using as a bench cover, roll up the ends to make little arm rests.

FOR THE BEDROLL

Holding a suitable number of ends together, make 79ch.

Row 1: 1dc in second ch from hook, 1dc in each ch to end, turn. (78 sts)

Rows 2–24: 1ch, 1dc in each st to end, turn.

Fasten off.

FINISHING

Weave in all loose ends and gently block to measurements.

PATTERN NOTES

• The bedroll is worked in rows holding several ends of yarn together to make a super-thick yarn. As you start to run out of one yarn, grab the next ball and tie the ends together with a reef knot and continue crocheting – the stitch pattern is super-easy so you can concentrate on playing around with yarn and colours.
• The turning chain does not count as a stitch throughout.

SKILL LEVEL

★☆☆

SIZE

One size: 50cm (20in) wide x 208cm (82in) long

YOU WILL NEED

Yarn

You will need a total of 1100g (44 oz) of yarn in any weight and thickness you like. If using super chunky yarn you will need to hold 4 ends together. For DK weight yarns you will need approximately 8 ends held together. The sample uses a mixture of super chunky and DK yarns, holding 5 ends together.

How many strands?

Follow the guide given above or use your judgement when mixing and matching yarns.

Hooks & Notions

25mm (US U/50) crochet hook

Large-eyed tapestry needle

TENSION

Tension is not critical but adjust the hook size to produce a firm yet flexible fabric.

ABBREVIATIONS

See page 9.

CABLE STITCH BLANKET

You'll probably gather from most of the patterns in the book that I'm not a very patient person – if it can't be made in a single evening, and I don't get instant gratification, then I'm not interested! This *is not* one of those patterns, having grown out of a desire to have something to snuggle under whilst curled up on the sofa as the autumn evenings grow chillier.

SKILL LEVEL
★ ★ ★

SIZE
One size: 91cm (36in) wide x 178cm (70in) long

YOU WILL NEED
Yarn
Cygnet, Seriously Chunky (super chunky weight; 100% acrylic)
- 20 x 100g (3½ oz) balls (48m / 52yds per ball) in shade 288 Cream (**A**)
- 2 x 100g (3½ oz) balls (48m / 52yds per ball) in shade 4888 Burnt Orange (**B**)
- 2 x 100g (3½ oz) balls (48m / 52yds per ball) in shade 4884 Barley (**C**)

How many strands?
Work with a single strand of each yarn.

Hooks & Notions
25mm (US U/50) crochet hook
Large-eyed tapestry needle

TENSION
Tension is not critical but adjust the hook size to produce a flexible fabric.

ABBREVIATIONS
See page 9.

FOR THE BLANKET
Holding a single strand of yarn A, make 47ch.
Row 1 (WS): 1dc in second ch from hook, 1dc in each ch to end, turn. (46 sts)
Row 2 (RS): 1ch, 1dc in each of next 12 sts, join yarn B and work 1FPtr in each of next 2 sts, using yarn A, 1dc in next st, using B, 1FPtr in each of next 2 sts, using A, 1dc in each of next 12 sts, join yarn C and work 1FPtr in each of next 2 sts, using A, 1dc in next st, using C, 1FPtr in each of next 2 sts, using A, 1dc in each of next 12 sts, turn.
Row 3: Using yarn A only, 1ch, 1dc in each st to end, turn.
Row 4: Repeat Row 2, but work the FPtr sts around the tr sts into the **second** row below.
Row 5: Repeat Row 3.
Row 6: 1ch, 1dc in each of first 12 sts, *using B and working FPtr sts as establised into **second** row below, work a cable over the next 5 sts as follows: 1FPtr in fourth st, 1FPtr in fifth st, using A work 1dc in third st, using B work 1FPtr in first st, 1FPtr in second st*, using A work 1dc in each of next 12 sts; rep from * to * using C for the second cable, using A work 1dc in each of next 12 sts, turn.

pattern continued overleaf

PATTERN NOTES
- There is no need to fasten off each shade as you change colours, you can simply carry the yarn across the back of your work taking care not to get in a tangle.

Row 7: Using yarn A only, 1ch, 1dc in each st to end, turn.

Rows 8–84: Repeat Rows 2–7 a further 14 times, always working the FPtr sts into the **second** row below.

Row 85: Using yarn A only, 1ch, 1dc in each st to end. Fasten off.

FOR THE BORDER

For the shorter top and bottom edges, join yarn B at the corner of the blanket and work 1 sl st in each st across.

For both longer side edges, join yarn C at the corner of the blanket and work 1 sl st in each row to end.

FINISHING

Weave in all loose ends and gently block to measurements.

TEA COSY

Being British, an obsession with tea comes as standard. In my kitchen cabinets you will find chilli choco tea, fresh mint tea, camomile tea, lavender tea, white tea, chai tea and good old-fashioned 'builders' tea. What all of these require is a good old fashioned tea pot. And what does a good old fashioned tea pot need? A good old fashioned tea cosy! I could have selected a tasteful palette but I found myself overwhelmed with the desire to have a rainbow cosy. With pompoms. I love it.

SKILL LEVEL
★★☆

SIZE
One size: 26cm (10in) diameter x 18cm (7in) tall

YOU WILL NEED
Yarn
Cygnet, Seriously Chunky (super chunky weight; 100% acrylic)
- 1 x 100g (3½ oz) ball (48m / 52yds per ball) in shade 4884 Barley (**A**)
- 1 x 100g (3½ oz) ball (48m / 52yds per ball) in shade 350 Russet (**C**)
- 1 x 100g (3½ oz) ball (48m / 52yds per ball) in shade 1206 Bright Red (**E**)
- 1 x 100g (3½ oz) ball (48m / 52yds per ball) in shade 5410 Magenta (**F**)
- 1 x 100g (3½ oz) ball (48m / 52yds per ball) in shade 708 Cornflower (**G**)

Wool and the Gang, Crazy Sexy Wool, (super chunky weight; 100% Peruvian wool)
- 1 x 200g (7 oz) ball (80m / 87yds) in shade Fireball Orange (**B**)
- 1 x 200g (7 oz) ball (80m / 87yds) in shade Candy Red (**D**)

DMC, Groovy (super chunky; 55% wool, 45% microfibre)
- 1 x 100g (3½ oz) ball (73m / 80yds per ball) in shade 07 Blue (**H**)

DMC, Nordic Spirit Ottowa (super chunky; 50% wool, 50% acrylic)
- 1 x 50g (1¾ oz) ball (29m /32yds per ball) in shade 082 Green (**I**)

DMC, Nordic Spirit Aurora (super chunky; 50% wool, 50% acrylic)
- 1 x 50g (1¾ oz) ball (29m /32yds per ball) in shade 1310 Carnival (**J**)

Optional aran weight yarn for pompoms

How many strands?
Work with two strands held together (one from each end of the ball).

Hooks & Notions
25mm (US U/50) crochet hook

Large-eyed tapestry needle

Pompom maker or cardboard

TENSION
Tension is not critical but adjust the hook size to produce a firm yet flexible fabric.

ABBREVIATIONS
See page 9.

FOR THE COSY

Holding two strands of yarn A together (one from each end of the ball), make a magic ring (see page 103).

Round 1: Work 5dc into the ring, join with sl st in first dc. (5 sts)

Round 2: Change to yarn B, 1ch, 2dc in each st around, join with sl st in first dc. (10 sts)

Round 3: Change to yarn C, 1ch, *2dc in next st, 1dc in next st; rep from * around, join with sl st in first dc. (15 sts)

Round 4: Change to yarn D, 1ch, *2dc in next st, 1dc in each of next 2 sts; rep from * around, **do not join the round**, turn. (20 sts)

Working in rows, change to yarn E and continue as follows:

Row 1: 1ch, 1dc in each st to end, turn. (20 sts)

Row 2: Change to yarn F and repeat Row 1.

Row 3: Change to yarn G and repeat Row 1.

Row 4: Change to yarn H and repeat Row 1.

Row 5: Change to yarn I and repeat Row 1.

Row 6: Change to yarn J and repeat Row 1.

Fasten off.

FINISHING

Weave in all loose ends and gently block to measurements.

Hand stitch each end of Rows 9 and 10 together to secure a slot for the handle of the tea pot. The stitch pattern of the crochet should be large enough for you to push the spout through on the opposite side.

Make as many or as few pompoms as you like for the top and stitch in place. I have experimented making pompoms with chunky yarn, but they just don't get the right sort of 'fluff', so I used regular DK weight yarn for mine.

MAKING THE POMPOMS

Use oddments of DK weight yarn from your stash for the pompoms. Hold several strands of different colours and textures together for a fun and fabulous finish!

CANDY SKULL RUG

Halloween is a big event in our house; any excuse to make costumes and dress the house up is fine by me. Last year our theme was the Mexican Day of the Dead festival and I started making this rug just three days before the big event, getting out of bed at 4am on Halloween to finish it! This is not a project for the faint-hearted, but it is so absolutely worth the effort and, although I made it for Halloween, it was never packed away and has pride of place in my craft room.

SKILL LEVEL

SIZE
One size: 92cm (36in) diameter

YOU WILL NEED
Yarn
Boodles, Textile Yarn (super chunky weight; upcycled reclaimed fabric)
- 2 x 450g (16 oz) cones in shade White (**A**)
- 1 x 450g (16 oz) cones in shade Black (**B**)
- 1 x 450g (16 oz) cones in shade Blue (**C**)
- 1 x 450g (16 oz) cones in shade Soft Red (**D**)
- 1 x 450g (16 oz) cones in shade Lime Green (**E**)

How many strands?
Work with one strand of yarn.

Hooks & Notions
25mm (US U/50) crochet hook
Large-eyed tapestry needle

TENSION
Tension is not critical but adjust the hook size to produce a firm fabric.

ABBREVIATIONS
See page 9.

FOR THE EYES (make 2 alike)
Holding a single strand of yarn B, make 3ch, join with sl st in first ch to form a ring.
Round 1: 1ch, 6dc in ring, join with sl st in first st. (6 sts)
Round 2: 1ch, 2dc in each st around, join with sl st in first st. (12 sts)
Fasten off yarn B and join yarn D.
Round 3: 1ch, (1dc, 1tr, 1dc) in first st, sl st in next st, *(1dc, 1tr, 1dc) in next st, sl st in next st; rep from * to end, join with sl st in first st.
Fasten off yarn D and join yarn E.
Round 4: 1ch, miss 1 st, *1dc in next st, 1ch, miss 1 st, 1tr in next st, 1ch, miss 1 st; rep from * to end, join with sl st in first st.
Fasten off yarn E, join yarn A.
Round 5: 1ch, 1dc in each of next 3 sts, 2dc in next st, *1dc in each of next 4 sts, 2dc in next st; rep from * to end, join with sl st in first st.
Fasten off and weave in ends.

FOR THE NOSE
Holding a single strand of yarn B, make 3ch, join with sl st in first ch to form a ring.
Round 1: 1ch, 7dc in ring, join with sl st in first st. (7 sts)
Round 2: 1ch, (1dc, 1tr, 1dc) in first st, 1dc in each of next 2 sts, (1dc, 1ch, 1dc) in next st, 1dc in each of next 2 sts, (1dc, 1tr, 1dc) in last st, join with sl st in first st.
Fasten off and weave in ends.

pattern continued overleaf

PATTERN NOTES
- The rug is constructed from separate pieces for the eyes, nose and mouth before stitching them together and crocheting around to finish.

FOR THE MOUTH

Holding a single strand of yarn A, make 15ch.

Row 1: 1dc in second ch from hook, 1dc in next 6ch, leaving yarn A attached change to yarn C, work 1dc in next ch, fasten off yarn C, change back to yarn A, work 1dc in each of next 6ch, turn. (14 sts)

Row 2: 3ch (counts as 1tr), miss first st, 1tr in each st to end, turn.

Row 3: 1ch, 1dc in each st to end, working final stitch in top of turning chain, turn.

Row 4: 3ch (counts as 1tr), miss first st, 1tr in each st to end, turn.

Row 5: 1ch, 1dc in each st to end, working final stitch in top of turning chain, turn.

Row 6: 3ch (counts as 1tr), miss first st, 1tr in each of next 2 sts, 1dc in next st, sl st in each of next 6 sts, 1dc in next st, 1tr in each of next 3 sts.

Fasten off and weave in ends.

JOINING THE FEATURES

Lay the two eyes side-by-side so the stitches line up. Join together by sewing along five stitches.

Fit the nose in the space between the eyes with the pointed end at the top. Line it up with the eye edges by tucking the nose in between the eyes, so the eyes are touching and the nose sits neatly between them, and sew together along four stitches on either side of the nose.

With the yarn C stitch at the bottom, place the mouth under the nose and eyes. Starting at the eye socket, six stitches along from where you joined the nose, sew the eyes to the mouth along those six stitches on either side and along the nose.

Don't worry if yours hasn't sewn together quite like this, you can easily add or remove a couple of stitches when you start working the skull shape and make sure to add or remove the same number of stitches when working the border rounds.

FINISH THE SKULL

Join yarn C to the st at the top inner corner of the right eye. Work 3ch, 1tr in same sp, 1ch, 2tr in next dc at the inner corner of the left eye.

Fasten off.

MAKING SPACE
This rug gets very big and heavy, so you'll need to work this on the floor, or clear a large table if it's more comfortable.

FOR THE BORDER

Round 1: Join yarn B at bottom left corner of mouth. 1ch, 2dc in bottom left corner st, working along the bottom of the mouth, 1dc in each of next 2 sts, 1htr in each of next 2 sts, 1tr in each of next 3 sts, 1htr in each of next 2 sts, 1dc in each of next 3 sts, working up RH side, 2dc in tr row end, 1 tr in dc row end, 2dc in tr row end, 2dc in next dc row end, 1htr in next st, 1tr in next st, 1htr in next st, 1dc in each of next 5 sts, 2dc in next st, 1dc in each of next 4 sts, 1htr in each of next 2 sts, 1tr in each of next 6 sts, 1htr in each of next 2 sts, 1dc in each of next 4 sts, 2dc in next st, 1dc in each of next 5 sts, 1htr in next st, 1tr in next st, 1htr in next st, 2dc in next st, 6dc down LH side of mouth, working into row ends as for RH side.
Fasten off yarn B and join yarn D.

Round 2: 3ch (counts as tr), miss first st, 1tr in each of next 5 tr, 2tr in next st, *1tr in each of next 6 sts, 2tr in next st; rep from * to end, join with sl st in first st.
Fasten off yarn D and join yarn E.

Round 3: 3ch (counts as tr), miss first st, 1tr in each of next 6 tr, 2tr in next st, *1tr in each of next 7 sts, 2tr in next st; rep from * to end, join with sl st in first st.

Fasten off yarn E and join yarn C.

Round 4: 3ch (counts as tr), miss first st, 1tr in each of next 7 tr, 2tr in next st, *1tr in each of next 8 sts, 2tr in next st; rep from * to end, join with sl st in first st.
Fasten off yarn C and join yarn B.

Round 5: 3ch (counts as tr), miss first st, 1tr in each of next 8 tr, 2tr in next st, *1tr in each of next 9 sts, 2tr in next st; rep from * to end, join with sl st in first st.
Fasten off yarn B and join yarn A.

Round 6: 3ch (counts as tr), miss first st, 1tr in each of next 9 tr, 2tr in next st, *1tr in each of next 10 sts, 2tr in next st; rep from * to end, join with sl st in first st.

Round 7: Continuing with yarn A, 3ch (counts as tr), miss first st, 1tr in each of next 10 tr, 2tr in next st, *1tr in each of next 11 sts, 2tr in next st; rep from * to end, join with sl st in first st.
Fasten off.

FINISHING
Weave in all loose ends and gently block to measurements.

GRANNY BLANKET

This blanket is testament to the obsessive-compulsive hold that crochet has over me! It started as a cushion cover, a nice, easy way to use up some of the super chunky yarn left over from other projects. But then I raided the stash, and excavated a glorious spectrum and variety of colourful yarns in a whole range of textures. Two squares quickly became six, which became twelve, and at big hook crochet scale, twelve granny squares makes a blanket!

SKILL LEVEL

★★☆

SIZE
One size: 125 x 178cm (50 x 70in)

YOU WILL NEED
Yarn
1.4kg (3lb) of yarn – any thickness and texture is suitable.

How many strands?
The sample blanket used a whole random selection of yarns, which I mixed and matched to create a suitable thickness for the 25mm (US U/50) crochet hook. Use your judgement and play with all your leftovers to achieve a suitable thickness.

Hooks & Notions
25mm (US U/50) crochet hook
Large-eyed tapestry needle

TENSION
Each granny square measures 43cm (17in).

ABBREVIATIONS
See page 9.

FOR EACH GRANNY SQUARE (make 12)
Holding a suitable number of strands together, make 4ch, sl st in first ch to join.

Round 1: 3ch (counts as first st throughout), working into the circle, 3tr, (3ch, 4tr) 3 times, 3ch, sl st in top of first 3ch of the round to join, changing colour as you work the final pull through. (4 ch-sp)

Round 2: 3ch, 1tr in each of next 3 sts, *(2tr, 3ch, 2tr) in ch-sp, 1tr in each of next 4 sts; rep from * twice more, (2tr, 3ch, 2tr) in ch-sp, sl st in top of first 3ch of the round to join, changing colour as you work the final pull through.

Round 3: 3ch, 1tr in each of next 5 sts, *(2tr, 3ch, 2tr) in ch-sp, 1tr in each of next 8 sts; rep from * twice more, (2tr, 3ch, 2tr) in ch-sp, 1tr in each of next 2 sts, sl st in top of first 3ch of the round to join, changing colour as you work the final pull through.

Round 4: 3ch, 1tr in each of next 7 sts, *(2tr, 3ch, 2tr) in ch-sp, 1tr in each of next 12 sts; rep from * twice more, (2tr, 3ch, 2tr) in ch-sp, 1tr in each of next 4 sts, sl st in top of first 3ch of the round to join. Fasten off.

pattern continued overleaf

PATTERN NOTES
- To change colours for each round, work the pull-through of the joining sl st in the colour for the next round.
- When making multi-coloured granny squares you can have a lot of ends to weave in before joining the blanket together. Work over the ends from the previous round with the new colour to make it less of a chore at the end.

ADJUSTING COLOURS
*Choose contrasting colours for
a bold finish or gather a palette
of co-ordinating shades for
a more subtle look.*

ADJUSTING SIZE

*Adjust the number of squares
to make the blanket smaller
or larger. For example, two
squares will make a fabulous
crib blanket or stitch them
together for a cushion cover.*

FINISHING

Weave in all loose ends and gently block each square to the given measurement – this will make it much easier to join them together and creates a neat finish.

There are many different methods for joining granny squares together but I found this technique resulted in a flat seam. I used one colour to join all seams as follows:

Lay the squares, right side up, in the configuration you would like. Insert the hook through the corner ch of the left hand square, then through the corner ch of the right hand square, using one strand of yarn, work a sl st through both thicknesses. Repeat in the next st along and keep going until you have joined one row of squares.

Once all the squares are joined, work a border of double crochet around the entire blanket.

Weave in any remaining ends and wrap yourself up in it!

STRIPED YARN BASKET

What does every crocheter need besides a crochet hook? Yarn! And if you have yarn, you need somewhere to keep it all together, and this basket does exactly that. After all, what could be better than a basket made of yarn to store your yarn in?!

SKILL LEVEL

SIZE
One size: 38cm (15in) wide x 25cm (10in) tall

YOU WILL NEED
Yarn
Tek Tek, T-shirt Yarn (super chunky weight; 100% cotton)
- 1 x 1kg (35 oz) cone (190m / 208yds per cone) in shade Light Brown (**A**)
- 1 x 1kg (35 oz) cone (190m / 208yds per cone) in shade Dark Brown (**B**)
- 1 x 1kg (35 oz) cone (190m / 208yds per cone) in shade White (**C**)

How many strands?
I found this brand of yarn varies enormously in thickness so it is best to use your judgement. For the sample I held both **A** and **B** together but **C** was much thicker and worked perfectly as a single strand.

Hooks & Notions
25mm (US U/50) crochet hook

Locking stitch marker

Large-eyed tapestry needle

TENSION
Tension is not critical but adjust the hook size to produce a firm fabric.

ABBREVIATIONS
See page 9.

FOR THE BASKET
Holding a strand each of yarn A and B together, make a magic ring (see page 103).

Round 1: 6dc into the ring, place marker for beginning of round. (6 sts)

Round 2: *1dc in next st, join C and work 1dc in same st; rep from * around. (12 sts)

Round 3: *Using A&B, 2dc in next st, using C work 1dc in next st; rep from * around. (18 sts)

Round 4: *Using A&B, 2dc in next st, 1dc in next st, using C work 1dc in next st; rep from * around. (24 sts)

Round 5: *Using A&B, 2dc in next st, 1dc in each of next 2 sts, using C work 1dc in next st; rep from * around. (30 sts)

Round 6: *Using A&B, 2dc in next st, 1dc in each of next 3 sts, using C work 1dc in next st; rep from * around. (36 sts)

Round 7: *Using A&B, 2dc in next st, 1dc in each of next 4 sts, using C work 1dc in next st; rep from * around. (42 sts)

Round 8: *Using A&B, 2dc in next st, 1dc in each of next 5 sts, using C work 1dc in next st; rep from * around. (48 sts)

pattern continued overleaf

PATTERN NOTES
- You will only need approximately 500g (17½ oz) of yarns A and B and 25g (1 oz) of yarn C.
- Wind yarn C into six smaller balls and use one for each diagonal stripe. To get a neat white line, when you switch yarns work the yarn over with white, pull through and finish the stitch using the brown. Don't fasten anything off, just pick up the white each time you get to that line.
- This project is worked in a spiral – use the stitch marker to keep track of the start of the round, moving it up as you complete a round.

Round 9: *Using A&B, 2dc in next st, 1dc in each of next 6 sts, using C work 1dc in next st; rep from * around. (54 sts)

Round 10: *Using A&B, 1dc in each of next 8 sts, using C work 1dc in next st; rep from * around.

Rounds 11–19: Repeat Round 10 a further 9 times. Continue as follows to make the handles:

Round 20: *5ch, miss 4 sts, 1dc in fifth st, 1dc in each of next 22 sts keeping in pattern; rep from * once more.

Round 21: *Work 5dc around the ch of previous round, 1dc in each of next 22 sts keeping in pattern; rep from * once more. Fasten off all ends.

FINISHING
Weave in all loose ends, weaving the white yarn back along the white stitches on the inside of the basket.

STAYING UNTANGLED
• *Things can get a little bit tangled with so many balls of yarn, but if you position the brown yarns on one side of your lap and the white on the other this should help keep things in order.*
• *Use different shades of yarn for each stripe to create a truly multi-coloured basket.*

APPLE DOORSTOP

This project was a flash of inspiration at bedtime and my husband found me rummaging around in my craft room for a crochet hook and suitable yarn. I was prepared to sit crocheting into the night, but in the end it took less than 30 minutes to make – my idea of an instant gratification project!

FOR THE APPLE

Start by pouring the rice into the plastic bag and tie it securely. You will gradually crochet around this shape to create the apple, working from the top downwards as follows:

Holding two strands of yarn A, and using the 25mm (US U/50) hook, make a magic ring (see page 103).

Round 1: 1ch, 6dc into the ring, sl st in first dc to join. (6 sts)

Round 2: 1ch, 2dc in each st around, sl st in first dc to join. (12 sts)

Round 3: 1ch, *2dc in each of next 2 sts, 1dc in next st; rep from * to end, sl st in first dc to join. (18 sts)

Round 4: 1ch, 1dc in each st around, sl st in first dc to join.

Round 5: 1ch, 1dc in each of next 16 sts, dc2tog, sl st in first dc to join. (17 sts)

Round 6: 1ch, 1dc in each of next 7 sts, dc2tog, 1dc in each of next 8 sts, sl st in first dc to join. (16 sts)

Round 7: 1ch, dc2tog, 1dc in each of next 14 sts, sl st in first dc to join. (15 sts)

Round 8: 1ch, 1dc in each of next 6 sts, dc2tog, 1dc in each of last 7 sts, sl st in first dc to join. (14 sts)

Place the rice bag into the beginnings of the crochet apple and continue as follows to close the bottom section.

Round 9: To create a firm base for the apple, work BLO for this round only, 1ch, 1dc in next st, *dc2tog, 1dc in next st; rep from * to last st, 1dc in next st, sl st in first dc to join. (10 sts)

Round 10: 1ch, dc2tog around, sl st in first dc to join. (5 sts)

Fasten off.

pattern continued overleaf

SKILL LEVEL

★★☆

SIZE

One size: 51cm (20in) circumference x 18cm (7in) tall

YOU WILL NEED

Yarn

Cygnet, Seriously Chunky (super chunky weight; 100% acrylic)

- 1 x 100g (3½ oz) balls (48m / 52yds per ball) in shade 1206 Bright Red (**A**)
- 1 x 100g (3½ oz) balls (48m / 52yds per ball) in shade 3583 Chocolate (**B**)

Red Heart, Shimmer (light worsted weight; 97% acrylic, 3% polyester)

- 1 x 100g (3½ oz) balls (256m / 280yds per ball) in shade 07 Lime (**C**)

How many strands?

Work with two strands each of yarn **A** and **B**, and four strands of yarn **C** held together.

Hooks & Notions

25mm (US U/50) crochet hook

9mm (US M/13) crochet hook

Large-eyed tapestry needle

1kg (2.2lb) bag of rice

Strong, non-biodegradable clear plastic bag

TENSION

Tension is not critical but adjust the hook size to produce a firm fabric.

ABBREVIATIONS

See page 9.

FOR THE STALK

Holding 2 strands of yarn B together, and using the 9mm (US M/13) hook, make 5ch.

Row 1: Sl st in second ch from hook, sl st in each of next 4ch.

Fasten off leaving a long tail for joining the stalk to the apple.

FOR THE LEAF

Holding 4 strands of yarn C together, and using the 9mm (US M/13) hook, make 6ch.

Row 1: Sl st in second ch from hook, 1dc in next ch, 1htr in each of next 3 sts, sl st in same st as last htr.

Fasten off leaving a long tail for joining the leaf to the apple.

FINISHING

Weave in the ends of the apple.

Stitch the stalk and leaf in place at the top of the apple with the BLO round towards the bottom.

FRUITY DOORSTOPS

• *Use the basic shape with different colours and yarns to create other fruity doorstops for use around the home – green apples, oranges, peaches and plums would all look great.*

• *If you're handy with a needle and thread you could make a fabric bag in a matching colour to hold the rice filler.*

FAUX KNIT CUSHION

I have tried knitting and it just doesn't 'click' for me in the way crochet does, but there is something about knitted stocking stitches I find so visually appealing. After trawling the internet for what seemed like days, I found a few tutorials for a stocking stitch style fabric created using a crochet hook. This cushion cover is the first of what I know will be many experiments with this stitch.

FOR THE CUSHION COVER

Holding 6 strands of yarn A together, and using the 23mm hook, make 37ch, sl st in first ch to join, taking care not to twist.

Round 1: 2ch (does not count as st throughout), 1htr in third ch from hook, 1htr in each ch to end, sl st in first htr to join. (37 sts)

Rounds 2–7: 2ch, 1htr in each 'hidden' st (see Pattern Notes) around, sl st in first htr to join.
Fasten off yarn A and join yarn B.

Round 8: 2ch, 1htr in each 'hidden' st around, sl st in first htr to join.
Fasten off yarn B and rejoin yarn A.

Rounds 9–10: 1htr in each 'hidden' st around, sl st in first htr to join.
Fasten off yarn A and rejoin yarn B.

pattern continued overleaf

PATTERN NOTES

- **To create the Faux Knit stitch:** The cushion cover is worked in half treble crochet. However, rather than working into the top 2 strands of the previous row as usual, work the stitch into the strand of yarn just below them at the back of the fabric. This is referred to as the 'hidden' stitch throughout the pattern and will make the 'V' of the top 2 strands roll forwards to the front of the work, producing the faux stocking effect.
- The 2ch at the start of each round does not count as a stitch.
- The cushion cover can be made using a 25mm (US U/50) crochet hook, but omit 1ch from the foundation chain.

SKILL LEVEL
★★☆

SIZE
One size: 45cm (18in) square

YOU WILL NEED
Yarn
Red Heart, Shimmer (DK weight; 97% acrylic, 3% polyester)
- 6 x 100g (3½ oz) balls (256m / 280yds per ball) in shade 07 Lime (**A**)

Wool and the Gang, Crazy Sexy Wool, (super chunky weight; 100% Peruvian wool)
- 3 x 200g (7 oz) balls (80m / 87yds per ball) in shade Fireball Orange (**B**)

How many strands?
Work with six strands of yarn **A** held together. When yarn **B** is used, work with only one strand.

Hooks & Notions
23mm crochet hook

Large-eyed tapestry needle

45cm (18in) square cushion insert

TENSION
Tension is not critical but adjust the hook size to produce a flexible fabric.

ABBREVIATIONS
See page 9.

Round 11: 2ch, 1htr in each 'hidden' st around, sl st in first htr to join.

Fasten off yarn B and join yarn A.

Rounds 12–18: 2ch, 1htr in each 'hidden' st around, sl st in first htr to join.

Round 19: 1ch, work 1dc in each 'hidden' st around, sl st in first dc to join.

Fasten off.

FINISHING

Weave in loose ends and gently block to measurements.

Slip stitch the two sides of the cushion cover together at one end, inserting the hook through both layers and working one sl st for each stitch along. Place the cushion inner inside the cover, then slip stitch along the other end in the same way to close.

Fasten off and weave in any remaining ends.

LARGER CUSHIONS

The cover will stretch to fit a slightly larger cushion but I recommend covering the cushion form in a matching fabric as it will be visible through the weave of the stitches. You could use a brightly coloured fabric for a pop of contrast!

TATTOO RUG

I have my sister to thank for the inspiration behind this project. She has a beautiful heart-shaped rag rug that I have coveted for years. After spending hours pondering what motifs to place on my crochet version, I realized the answer had been staring me in the face all along, and worked from the tattoo on my inner wrist created by my tattooist sister. The chenille yarn can be a bit tricky to work with, but makes the softest fabric for tucking your toes into!

SKILL LEVEL
★★☆

SIZE
One size: 68.5cm (27in) across x 61cm (24in) length

YOU WILL NEED
Yarn
James C Brett, Flutterby Chenille (chunky weight; 100% polyester)
- 3 x 100g (3½ oz) balls (175m / 192yds per ball) in shade B12 Fondant (**A**)

Small quantities of DK weight yarn in the following shades: Grey (**B**), Pink (**C**), Peach (**D**), Green (**E**)

How many strands?
Work with 3 strands of yarn **A** held together. For the embellishments hold a single strand of the DK weight yarn.

Hooks & Notions
25mm (US U/50) crochet hook

5mm (US H/8) hook

Large-eyed tapestry needle

100cm (39in) square of rug canvas

Tailor's chalk

Pins

TENSION
Tension is not critical but adjust the hook size to produce a firm yet flexible fabric.

ABBREVIATIONS
See page 9.

FOR THE RUG
Holding 3 strands of yarn A together, and using the 25mm (US U/50) hook, make a magic ring (see page 103).

Round 1: 1ch, 5dc into the ring, sl st in first dc to join. (5 sts)

Round 2: 1ch, 2dc in each st around, sl st in first dc to join. (10 sts)

Round 3: 1ch, (1dc, 4tr) in first st, 1dc in each of next 3 sts, (1dc, 1ch, 1tr, 1ch, 1dc) in next st, 1dc in each of next 3 sts, (4tr, 1dc) in next st, 1dc in last st, sl st in first dc to join.

Round 4: 1ch, 1dc in first st, 2tr in next st, 3tr in next st, 1tr in next st, 1dc in each of next 5 sts, 1dc in ch-sp, 1ch, (1tr, 1ch, 1tr) in next st, 1ch, 1dc in ch-sp, 1dc in each of next 5 sts, 1tr in next st, 3tr in next st, 2tr in next st, 1dc in next st, 1dc in last st, sl st in first dc to join.

Round 5: 1ch, 1dc in first st, 1tr in next st, 2tr in each of next 4 sts, 1tr in next st, 1dc in each of next 6 sts, 1dc in ch-sp, 1dc in next st, (1dc, 3ch, 1dc) in ch-sp, 1dc in next st, 1dc in ch-sp, 1dc in each of next 6 sts, 1tr in next st, 2tr in each of next 4 sts, 1tr in next st, 1dc in each of next 2 sts, sl st in first dc to join.

Round 6: 1ch, 1dc in first st, 1tr in next st, 2tr in each of next 3 sts, 1tr in each of next 2 sts, 2tr in next st, 1tr in each of next 12 sts, (2tr, 1ch, 2tr) in ch-sp, 1tr in each of next 12 sts, 2tr in next st, 1tr in each of next 2 sts, 2tr in each of next 3 sts, 1tr in next st, 1dc in each of next 2 sts, sl st in first dc to join.

pattern continued overleaf

PATTERN NOTES
- Make each individual embellishment motif and arrange them as desired before stitching into place. Don't worry about weaving in the ends of the motifs as they can be used to attach the motifs to the rug.

Round 7: 1ch, 1dc in first st, 1tr in each of next 3 sts, 2tr in next st, 1tr in next st, 2tr in next st, 1tr in each of next 3 sts, 2tr in next st, 1tr in next st, 2tr in next st, 1tr in each of next 9 sts, 2tr in next st, 1tr in each of next 3 sts, (1tr, 1ch, 1tr) in ch-sp, 1tr in each of next 3 sts, 2tr in next st, 1tr in each of next 9 sts, 2tr in next st, 1tr in next st, 2tr in next st, 1tr in each of next 3 sts, 2tr in next st, 1tr in next st, 2tr in next st, 1tr in each of next 3 sts, 1dc in each of next 2 sts, sl st in first dc to join.

Round 8: 1ch, 1dc in first st, 1tr in each of next 3 sts, 2tr in next st, 1tr in next st, 2tr in next st, 1tr in each of next 2 sts, 2tr in next st, 1tr in each of next 3 sts, 2tr in next st, 1tr in each of next 2 sts, 2tr in next st, 1tr in each of next 15 sts, (1dc, 1ch, 1dc) in ch-sp, 1tr in each of next 15 sts, 2tr in next st, 1tr in each of next 2 sts, 2tr in next st, 1tr in each of next 3 sts, 2tr in next st, 1tr in each of next 2 sts, 2tr in next st, 1tr in next st, 2tr in next st, 1tr in each of next 3 sts, 1dc in each of next 2 sts, sl st in first dc to join.
Fasten off.

FINISHING

Weave in all loose ends and gently block to measurements.

Lay the rug on the backing material and using the tapestry needle and a length of chenille yarn, stitch it in place. I used blanket stitch as this holds the edges neatly in place. Trim the fabric into any shape you like – the sample has a pretty scalloped edging which I drew on with tailor's chalk before cutting.

FOR THE MOTIF EMBELLISHMENTS

Anchor Top hoop
Holding a single strand of yarn B, and using the 5mm (US H/8) hook, make 20ch, sl st in first ch to join.
Round 1: 3ch, work 29tr around the chain loop, sl st in top of first 3ch to join.
Fasten off.

Anchor Central post
Holding a single strand of yarn B, and using the 5mm (US H/8) hook, make 32ch.
Row 1: 1tr in fourth ch from hook, 1tr in each ch to end.
Fasten off.

Anchor Crossbar
Holding a single strand of yarn B, and using the 5mm (US H/8) hook, make 18ch.

Row 1: 1htr in second ch from hook, 1htr in each of next 15 ch, 1dc in last ch.
Fasten off.

Anchor Base
Holding a single strand of yarn B, and using the 5mm (US H/8) hook, make 39ch.
Row 1: Sl st in first ch from hook, 1dc in each of next 2 ch, 1htr in each of next 2 ch, 1tr in each of next 14 sts, (2tr, 1ch, 2tr) in next ch, 1tr in each of next 14 sts, 1htr in each of next 2 sts, 1dc in each of next 2 sts, sl st in last ch.
Fasten off.

Anchor base points (make 2 alike)
Holding a single strand of yarn B, and using the 5mm (US H/8) hook, make 9ch.
Row 1: Sl st in first ch from hook, sl st in next ch, 1dc in next ch, 1htr in next ch, (2tr, 1ch, 2tr) in next ch, 1htr in next ch, 1dc in next ch, sl st in last 2 sts.
Fasten off.

Vine
Holding a single strand of yarn E, and using the 5mm (US H/8) hook, make 60ch and fasten off. Adjust length as desired.

Leaf (make 3 alike)
Holding a single strand of yarn E, and using the 5mm (US H/8) hook, make 8ch.
Row 1: Sl st in first ch from hook, 1dc in next ch, 1htr in each of next 2 ch, 1tr in next 2 ch, 1htr in next ch, 4htr in last ch, working back up the other side of the foundation ch, 1htr in next ch, 1tr in each of next 2 ch, 1htr in each of next 2 ch, 1dc in next ch.
Fasten off.

Small Heart
Holding a single strand of yarn C, and using the 5mm (US H/8) hook, make a magic ring.
Round 1: 1ch, work 5dc into the ring, sl st in first dc to join. (5 sts)
Round 2: 1ch, 2dc in each st around, sl st in first dc to join. (10 sts)
Round 3: 1ch, (1dc, 4tr) in first st, 1tr in each of next 3 sts, (2tr, 1ch, 2tr) in next st, 1tr in each of next 3 sts, (4tr, 1dc) in next st, 1dc in last st, sl st in first dc to join.
Round 4: 1ch, 1dc in first st, 2tr in each of next 4 sts, 1tr in each of next 5 sts, (2tr, 1ch, 2tr) in ch-sp, 1tr in each of

next 5 sts, 2tr in each of next 4 sts, 1dc in next st, sl st in first dc to join.
Fasten off.

Rose

Holding a single strand of yarn D, and using the 5mm (US H/8) hook, make 55ch.
Row 1: 1dc in second ch from hook, 2ch, miss 1ch, *1dc in each of next 2 ch, 2ch, miss 1ch; rep from * to last ch, 1dc in last ch, turn.
Row 2: 2ch, 1htr in ch-sp, *miss 1 st, 6htr in ch-sp; rep from * to end.
Fasten off and coil up the rose, securing with a couple of stitches.

JOINING THE PIECES

Lay everything out as desired – I wrapped the vine around the central post of the anchor and pinned everything in place on the rug. Using the tapestry needle and the tail-ends of each motif, stitch all the elements into place.

Weave in any remaining ends.

HOUSE BOWL

An amazingly quick, but genuinely useful project that you can whip up in less than an hour. I have a compulsion to organise things by colour, so the contrast trim around the top works as an indicator for what goes in that particular bowl – this one was made to hold a whole variety of blue and green objects from pompom makers to nail varnish!

FOR THE BOWL
Holding a single strand of yarn A, and using the 23mm hook, make a magic ring (see page 103).
Round 1: 1ch (does not count as st throughout), 6dc into the ring, sl st in first dc to join. (6 sts)
Round 2: 1ch, 2dc in each st around, sl st in first dc to join. (12 sts)
Round 3: 1ch, *2dc in next st, 1dc in next st; rep from * around, sl st in first dc to join. (18 sts)
Round 4: 1ch, *2dc in next st, 1dc in each of next 2 sts; rep from * around, sl st in first dc to join. (24 sts)
Round 5: 1ch, *2dc in next st, 1dc in each of next 3 sts; rep from * around, sl st in first dc to join. (30 sts)
Rounds 6–7: 1ch, 1dc in each st around, sl st in first dc to join.
Fasten off yarn A.
Round 8: Join yarn B in any dc, and using the 6mm (US J/10) hook, work 3ch (counts as 1tr), 2tr in same dc, 3tr in each dc around, sl st in top of 3ch to join.
Fasten off.

FINISHING
Weave in all loose ends and gently steam block, taking care to maintain the shape of the bowl.

COLOUR CODED BOWLS
These bowls are perfect for use all around the house – designate a colour for each household member to tidy any stray odds and ends away into.

SKILL LEVEL
★ ☆ ☆

SIZE
One size: 27cm (11in) wide

YOU WILL NEED
Yarn
DMC, Neo Vintage Mia (super chunky weight; 80% microfibre, 20% wool)
  • 1 x 100g (3½ oz) ball (33m /36yds per ball) in shade 11 Natural (**A**)
Lion Brand, Baby's First (chunky weight; 55% acrylic, 45% cotton)
  • 1 x 100g (3½ oz) ball (110m /120yds per 100g) in shade 156 Beanstalk (**B**)

How many strands?
Work holding a single strand.

Hooks & Notions
23mm crochet hook
6mm (US J/10) crochet hook
Large-eyed tapestry needle

TENSION
Tension is not critical but adjust the hook size to produce a flexible fabric.

ABBREVIATIONS
See page 9.

RIPPLE BATH MAT

I hadn't crocheted a ripple pattern before starting this project but I'm of the opinion that the best way to learn is to just get in there and make something! The colour scheme neatly lends itself to the wavy, rippled water theme of the pattern. Turn over to page 90 to make a matching Towel Basket.

SKILL LEVEL

★★☆

SIZE

One size: 44cm (17in) tall x 70cm (27in) wide

YOU WILL NEED

Yarn

Tek Tek, T-shirt Yarn (super chunky; 100% cotton)

- 2 x 1kg (35 oz) cones (190m / 208yds per cone) in shade Navy Blue (**A**)
- 2 x 1kg (35 oz) cones (190m / 208yds per cone) in shade Bright Blue (**B**)
- 2 x 1kg (35 oz) cones (190m / 208yds per cone) in shade White (**C**)

How many strands?
Work with two strands held together.

Hooks & Notions

25mm (US U/50) crochet hook

Large-eyed tapestry needle

TENSION

Tension is not critical but adjust the hook size to produce a flexible fabric.

ABBREVIATIONS

See page 9.

FOR THE BATH MAT

Holding 2 strands of yarn A, make 35ch.

Row 1: 1tr in fourth ch from hook (missed 3ch counts as 1tr), 1tr in each of next 3 ch, *(1tr, 1ch, 1tr) in next ch, 1tr in each of next 5 ch, tr3tog (see Pattern Notes), 1tr in each of next 5 ch; rep from * once more, turn.
Fasten off yarn A and join yarn B.

Row 2: Working FLO for this row, 3ch (counts as 1tr), 1tr in first st, 1tr in each of next 3 sts, tr3tog, 1tr in each of next 5 sts, (1tr, 1ch, 1tr) in ch-sp, 1tr in each of next 5 sts, tr3tog, 1tr in each of next 5 sts, (1tr, 1ch, 1tr) in ch-sp, 1tr in each of next 4 sts, tr2tog, turn.
Fasten off yarn B and join yarn C.

Row 3: Working BLO for this row, 3ch (counts as 1tr), miss first st, tr2tog, 1tr in each of next 3 sts, (1tr, 1ch, 1tr) in ch-sp, 1tr in each of next 5 sts, tr3tog, 1tr in each of next 5 sts, (1tr, 1ch, 1tr) in ch-sp, 1tr in each of next 5 sts, tr3tog, 1tr in each of next 3 sts, 2tr in last st, turn.
Fasten off yarn C and join yarn A.

Row 4: As Row 2.
Fasten off yarn A and join yarn B.

Row 5: As Row 3.
Fasten off yarn B and join yarn C.

Rows 6–9: Continue changing colour as set and work Rows 2–3 twice more.

Row 10: Continuing with yarn C, 1ch, 1dc in each st across.
Fasten off.

FINISHING

Weave in all loose ends and gently block to measurements.

PATTERN NOTES

This pattern uses two special stitches as detailed below:

- **tr3tog:** *yrh, insert hook in next stitch, yrh, pull through stitch, yrh, pull through first two loops; rep from * twice more, yrh, pull through all four loops on hook. (1 loop remaining on hook; 2 stitches decreased)
- **tr2tog:** * yrh, insert hook in next stitch, yrh, pull through stitch, yrh, pull through first two loops; rep from * once more, yrh, pull through all three loops on hook. (1 loop remaining on hook; 1 stitch decreased)
- Turning chain counts as a stitch throughout and should be worked into as last stitch at end of row.

MADE TO LAST
Using two strands of jersey yarn together gives this mat really good durability.

TOWEL BASKET

My first job was as a curator at a craft museum and a gorgeous volunteer, an elderly lady called Jean, told me how she worked as a basket weaver during the Second World War. Her tales of weaving these huge baskets on the floor – until her hands were blistered but she was filled with a deep sense of satisfaction – were the inspiration for this much softer version. Be warned, though: you may find yourself on the floor finishing it as it gets too big for your lap!

SKILL LEVEL

SIZE
One size: 46cm (18in) wide x 46cm (18in) tall

YOU WILL NEED

Yarn
Tek Tek, T-shirt Yarn (super chunky weight; 100% cotton)
- 2 x 1kg (35 oz) cones (190m / 208yds per cone) in shade Bright Blue (**A**)
- 2 x 1kg (35 oz) cones (190m / 208yds per cone) in shade Navy Blue (**B**)
- 2 x 1kg (35 oz) cones (190m / 208yds per cone) in shade White (**C**)

How many strands?
Work with two strands held together.

Hooks & Notions
25mm (US U/50) crochet hook

Large-eyed tapestry needle

TENSION
Tension is not critical but adjust the hook size to produce a firm fabric.

ABBREVIATIONS
See page 9.

FOR THE BASKET
Holding 2 strands of yarn A, make a magic ring (see page 103).

Round 1: 1ch (does not count as st throughout), 6dc into the ring, sl st in first dc to join. (6 sts)

Round 2: 1ch, 2dc in each st around, sl st in first dc to join. (12 sts)

Round 3: 1ch, *2dc in next st, 1dc in next st; rep from * around, sl st in first dc to join. (18 sts)

Round 4: 1ch, *2dc in next st, 1dc in each of next 2 sts; rep from * around, sl st in first dc to join. (24 sts)

Round 5: 1ch, *2dc in next st, 1dc in each of next 3 sts; rep from * around, sl st in first dc to join. (30 sts)

Round 6: 1ch, *2dc in next st, 1dc in each of next 4 sts; rep from * around, sl st in first dc to join. (36 sts)

Round 7: 1ch, *2dc in next st, 1dc in each of next 5 sts; rep from * around, sl st in first dc to join. (42 sts)

Fasten off yarn A and join yarn B.

Round 8: 1ch, working FLO for this round only, work 1dc in each st around, sl st in first dc to join.

Round 9: 1ch, 2dc in first st, 1dc in each of next 20 sts, 2dc in next st, 1dc in each of next 20 sts, sl st in first dc to join. (44 sts)

Fasten off yarn B and join yarn C.

Round 10: 1ch, 1dc in each st around, sl st in first dc to join.

Round 11: 1ch, 1dc in each of next 11 sts, 2dc in next st, 1dc in each of next 21 sts, 2dc in next st, 1dc in each of next 10 sts, sl st in first dc to join. (46 sts)

Fasten off yarn C and rejoin yarn A.

Round 12: 1ch, 1dc in each st around, sl st in first dc to join.

Round 13: 1ch, 2dc in first st, 1dc in each of next 22 sts, 2dc in next st, 1dc in each of next 22 sts, sl st in first dc to join. (48 sts)

Fasten off yarn A and rejoin yarn B.

pattern continued overleaf

HANDY STORAGE

These sturdy baskets are brilliant for use all over the home – keep shoes, toys, yarn, pretty much anything in them!

Round 14: 1ch, 1dc in each st around, sl st in first dc to join.

Round 15: 1ch, 1dc in each of next 11 sts, 2dc in next st, 1dc in each of next 24 sts, 2dc in next st, 1dc in each of next 11 sts, sl st in first dc to join. (50 sts)
Fasten off yarn B and rejoin yarn C.

Round 16: 1ch, 1dc in each st around, sl st in first dc to join.

Round 17: 1ch, 2dc in first st, 1dc in each of next 24 sts, 2dc in next st, 1dc in each of next 24 sts, sl st in first dc to join. (52 sts)
Fasten off yarn C and rejoin yarn A.

Round 18: 1ch, 1dc in each st around, sl st in first dc to join.

Round 19: 1ch, 1dc in each of next 12 sts, 2dc in next st, 1dc in each of next 26 sts, 2dc in next st, 1dc in each of next 12 sts, sl st in first dc to join. (54 sts)
Fasten off yarn A and rejoin yarn B.

Round 20: 1ch, 1dc in each st around, sl st in first dc to join.

Round 21: 1ch, 2dc in first st, 1dc in each of next 26 sts, 2dc in next st, 1dc in each of next 26 sts, sl st in first dc to join. (56 sts)
Fasten off yarn B and rejoin yarn C.

Round 22: 1ch, 1dc in each st around, sl st in first dc to join.

Round 23: 1ch, 1dc in each of next 14 sts, 2dc in next st, 1dc in each of next 26 sts, 2dc in next st, 1dc in each of next 14 sts, sl st in first dc to join. (58 sts)
Fasten off yarn C and rejoin yarn A.

Rounds 24–25: 1ch, 1dc in each st around, sl st in first dc to join.

Round 26: 1ch, 1dc in each of next 10 sts, 8ch (handle made), miss 5 st, 1dc in each of next 24 sts, 8ch (handle made), miss 5 sts, 1dc in each of next 14 sts, sl st in first dc to join.

Round 27: 1ch, 1dc in each of next 10 sts, work 6dc around 8ch, 1dc in each of next 24 sts, work 6dc around 8ch, 1dc in each of next 14 sts, sl st in first dc to join. Fasten off.

FINISHING
Weave in all loose ends and gently steam block to finish.

DUVET BOLSTER

Like so many projects in this book, this came about out of necessity: in this case, a storage solution for all the spare single duvets and sleeping bags we seem to have in our little house! Fold the duvet in half and roll it up, then pop it in the crocheted bolster case. Not only is it neat and tidy, but you can then use it as, well, a bolster!

FOR THE BOLSTER ENDS (make 2 alike)
Holding 2 strands of yarn A, make a magic ring (see page 103).
Round 1: 1ch (does not count as st throughout), 6dc into the ring, sl st in first dc to join. (6 sts)
Round 2: 1ch, 2dc in each st around, sl st in first dc to join. (12 sts)
Round 3: 1ch, *2dc in next st, 1dc in next st; rep from * around, sl st in first dc to join. (18 sts)
Round 4: 1ch, *2dc in next st, 1dc in each of next 2 sts; rep from * around, sl st in first dc to join. (24 sts)
Round 5: 1ch, *2dc in next st, 1dc in each of next 3 sts; rep from * around, sl st in first dc to join. (30 sts)
Round 6: 1ch, *2dc in next st, 1dc in each of next 4 sts; rep from * around, sl st in first dc to join. (36 sts)
Fasten off.

FOR THE BOLSTER BODY
Holding 2 strands of yarn A, make 26ch.
Row 1: 1dc in second ch from hook, 1dc in each ch to end, turn. (25 sts)
Rows 2–47: 1ch, 1dc in each st to end, turn.
Fasten off yarn A, join yarn B.
Rows 48–49: 1ch, 1dc in each st to end, turn.
Fasten off yarn B, rejoin yarn A.
Rows 50–52: 1ch, 1dc in each st to end, turn.
Fasten off yarn A, rejoin yarn B.
Row 53: 1ch, 1dc in each st to end, turn.
Fasten off yarn B, rejoin yarn A.
Rows 54–56: 1ch, 1dc in each st to end, turn.
Fasten off yarn A, rejoin yarn B.
Row 57: 1ch, 1dc in each st to end, turn.
Fasten off.

SKILL LEVEL
★☆☆

SIZE
One size: 33cm (13in) wide x 79cm (31in) length, measured flat

YOU WILL NEED
Yarn
Lion Brand, Hometown USA (super chunky weight; 100% acrylic)
- 9 x 142g (5 oz) balls (74m / 81yds per ball) in shade LA Tan (**A**)
- 1 x 142g (5 oz) balls (74m / 81yds per ball) in shade Detroit Blue (**B**)

How many strands?
Work holding 2 strands together.

Hooks & Notions
25mm (US U/50) crochet hook
Large-eyed tapestry needle

TENSION
Tension is not critical but adjust the hook size to produce a firm yet flexible fabric.

ABBREVIATIONS
See page 9.

pattern continued overleaf

FINISHING

Weave in all loose ends and gently block to measurements.

In order to neatly hide the duvet inside the bolster cover, the body of the bolster must overlap itself as follows:

Take one end piece and wrap the body section around the edge of it, wrapping it round approximately 1½ times. Make sure the rows of yarn B of the body are on top. Using a length of yarn, roughly sew the end to the body and repeat for the other end.

Using yarn B, crochet the ends to the body by working double crochet through both the stitches of the bolster end and the row edges of the body section, then remove the 'basting' yarn you originally used to join the pieces together.

Fold the duvet in half, lengthways, roll it up and wriggle it into the bolster cover. You can always use a length of blue yarn to tie down the edges once it is in place.

FILLING THE BOLSTER
If you don't happen to have a spare single duvet or sleeping bag to stuff the bolster cover with, you will find bolster cushion inserts at your local craft store.

OWL RUG

In front of the fire, on the living room floor of my grandparent's house, was a rug that ran from shades of orange through to brown, and I originally picked the yarn for this project to make my own version. The design developed a life of its own and resulted in this lovely little owl who will look perfect greeting guests at the door or in front of your own fire.

SKILL LEVEL
★★☆

SIZE
One size: 40cm (16in) across x 52cm (21in) length

YOU WILL NEED
Yarn
Tek Tek, T-shirt Yarn (super chunky weight; 100% cotton)
- 1 x 1kg (35 oz) cone (190m / 208yds per cone) in shade Light Brown (**A**)
- 1 x 1kg (35 oz) cone (190m / 208yds per cone) in shade Dark Brown (**B**)
- 1 x 1kg (35 oz) cone (190m / 208yds per cone) in shade White (**C**)

Boodles, Textile Yarn (super chunky weight; upcycled reclaimed fabric)
- 1 x 450g (16 oz) cone in shade Yellow (**D**)
- 1 x 450g (16 oz) cone in shade Gold (**E**)
- 1 x 450g (16 oz) cone in shade Black (**F**)

How many strands?
I found this brand of yarn varies enormously in thickness from colour to colour, so use your judgement as to how many strands to crochet with. For the sample, I worked with two strands held together of all the shades apart from yarn B which was thick enough to work as a single strand.

Hooks & Notions
25mm (US U/50) crochet hook
Large-eyed tapestry needle

TENSION
Tension is not critical but adjust the hook size to produce a firm fabric.

ABBREVIATIONS
See page 9.

FOR THE BODY
Holding two strands of yarn E together, make a magic ring (see page 103).
Round 1: 1ch, 6dc into the ring, sl st in first dc to join. (6 sts)
Round 2: 1ch, 2dc in each st around, sl st in first dc to join. (12 sts)
Round 3: 1ch, *2dc in first st, 1dc in next st; rep from * to end, sl st in first dc to join. (18 sts)
Fasten off yarn E and join yarn A.
Round 4: 1ch, *2dc in first st, 1dc in each of next 2 sts; rep from * to end, sl st in first dc to join. (24 sts)
Round 5: 1ch, *2dc in first st, 1dc in each of next 3 sts; rep from * to end, sl st in first dc to join. (30 sts)
Fasten off yarn A and join yarn B.
Round 6: 1ch, *2dc in first st, 1dc in each of next 4 sts; rep from * to end, sl st in first dc to join. (36 sts)
Fasten off leaving a good length of yarn.

pattern continued overleaf

PATTERN NOTES
- The project does not use a full cone of each colour. The following quantities are a rough guide as to how much yarn is required: 100g (3½ oz) of A, 200g (7 oz) of B, 25g (1 oz) of C, 25g (1 oz) of D, 100g (3½ oz) of E, 25g (1 oz) of F.
- The rug is constructed from separate pieces for the body, eyes and beak before stitching them together and crocheting around to finish.

FOR THE EYES (make 2 alike)

Holding two strands of yarn F together, make a magic ring.

Round 1: 1ch, 6dc into the ring, sl st in first dc to join. (6 sts)

Fasten off yarn F and join yarn C.

Round 2: 1ch, 2dc in each st around, sl st in first dc to join. (12 sts)

Fasten off.

FOR THE BEAK

Holding two strands of yarn D together, make a magic ring.

Row 1: 3ch, (2tr, 3ch, 2tr) into the ring, 3ch, sl st into the ring.

Fasten off.

JOINING THE PIECES

Weave in all loose ends leaving the long tail on the body and join the sections as follows:

Step 1: Placing the beak so the 3ch-sp between the tr sts is at the bottom to form the point of the beak, join the eyes to the top corners of the beak at the sl st of each eye.

Step 2: Join yarn B at the top right corner of the beak – this is the stitch where you attached it to the right eye. Work 3ch, 1tr in 3ch of top right edge of beak, 2tr in magic ring of beak, 2tr in 3ch of top left edge of beak. Continuing around the left eye, miss the first st, 1dc in next st, *2dc in next st, 1dc in next st; rep from * to 1 st before the eye joins the beak, (1dc, 1ch, 1tr) in last st. 3ch behind the beak, (1tr, 1ch, 1dc) in equivalent stitch of right eye (just below where the beak is joined), *2dc in next st, 1dc in next st; rep from * until you are back to where you started, sl st in top of 3ch to join. Do not fasten off.

Step 3: Using the long tail from the body, join it to the head across 4 sts on each side of the beak and to the central 3ch behind the beak.

Step 4: Pick up where you stopped above the beak and work around the whole piece as follows: 3ch, 1tr in same st, 1tr in each of next 2 sts, 2tr in next st, miss 3 sts, 1dc in next 3 sts (working around the eye), 2dc in next st, (1dc, 1tr, 1ch, 1tr) in next st (ear point made), *1dc in each of next 2 sts, 2dc in next st, rep from * once more. Do not fasten off.

Step 5: Continue around the edge of the body as follows, beginning in the first body st that has not been joined to the eye: *1tr in each of next 5 sts, 2tr in next st; rep from * a further 3 times, 1tr in each of next 4 sts. Do not fasten off.

Step 6: Continue around right eye, beginning in the first eye st that has not been joined to the body: *2dc in next st, 1dc in each of next 2 sts; rep from * once more, (1tr, 1ch, 1tr, 1dc) in next st (ear point made), 2dc in next st, 1dc in each of next 3 sts, join with sl st in 3ch. Fasten off.

FINISHING

Weave in remaining ends and gently block to measurements.

A CHILD'S OWL

Create a brightly coloured owl to use in a child's playroom or for the den.

KITCHEN CHAIR CUSHION

One of my favourite thrift store finds was a pair of bentwood chairs, which have been transformed several times with a tin of paint. While being very pretty to look at, they are a tad uncomfortable so, once again, I grabbed my crochet hook and got to work making cushions to protect my behind when sitting down!

SKILL LEVEL
 ★ ☆ ☆

SIZE
One size: 35cm (14in) wide

YOU WILL NEED
Yarn
Sirdar, Big Softie (super chunky weight; 51% wool, 49% acrylic)
- 2 x 50g (1¾ oz) balls (45m / 49yds per ball) in shade 353 Downy (**A**)
- 2 x 50g (1¾ oz) balls (45m / 49yds per ball) in shade 357 Finn (**B**)
- 2 x 50g (1¾ oz) balls (45m / 49yds per ball) in shade 360 Blizzard (**C**)

How many strands?
Work holding two strands together.

Hooks & Notions
25mm (US U/50) crochet hook
Large-eyed tapestry needle

TENSION
Tension is not critical but adjust the hook size to produce a firm yet flexible fabric.

ABBREVIATIONS
See page 9.

FOR THE CUSHION
Holding 2 strands of yarn A, make a magic ring (see page 103).
Round 1: 1ch (does not count as st throughout), 5dc into the ring, sl st in first dc to join. (5 sts)
Round 2: 1ch, 2dc in each st around, sl st in first dc to join. (10 sts)
Fasten off 1 strand of yarn A and holding 1 strand of yarn A with 1 strand of yarn B, continue as follows:
Round 3: 1ch, *2dc in next st, 1dc in next st; rep from * around, sl st in first dc to join. (15 sts)
Fasten off yarn A and join a second strand of yarn B.
Round 4: 1ch, *2dc in next st, 1dc in each of next 2 sts; rep from * around, sl st in first dc to join. (20 sts)
Round 5: 1ch, *2dc in next st, 1dc in each of next 3 sts; rep from * around, sl st in first dc to join. (25 sts)
Fasten off 1 strand of yarn B and join 1 strand of yarn C.
Round 6: 1ch, *2dc in next st, 1dc in each of next 4 sts; rep from * around, sl st in first dc to join. (30 sts)
Fasten off yarn B and join a second strand of yarn C.
Round 7: 1ch, *2dc in next st, 1dc in each of next 5 sts; rep from * around, sl st in first dc to join. (35 sts)
Round 8: 1ch, *2dc in next st st, 1dc in each of next 6 sts; rep from * around, sl st in first dc to join. (40 sts)
Fasten off.

FINISHING
Weave in all loose ends and block to measurements.

FOR THE TIES (make 2 alike)
Cut a 24in (60cm) length in each shade of yarn. Holding the three strands together, fold them in half and loop through a stitch at the edge of the cushion, then pull the strands through the loop. Fasten to your chair and sit in comfort!

PATTERN NOTES
• By reversing yarns A and C, the given quantity of yarn will be sufficient to make two cushions.

INSTANT UPDATE
Change the cushions when you change the colour of the chairs for a quick and easy home decor update.

CROCHET TECHNIQUES

In this section, we explain how to master the simple crochet and sewing techniques that you need to make the projects in this book.

BASIC CROCHET TECHNIQUES

Holding the hook
Pick up your hook as though you are picking up a pen or pencil. Keeping the hook held loosely between your fingers and thumb, turn your hand so that the palm is facing up and the hook is balanced in your hand and resting in the space between your index finger and your thumb.

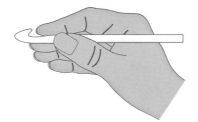

Making a slip knot
The simplest way is to make a circle with the yarn, so that the loop is facing downwards.

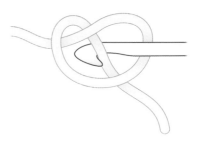

1 In one hand hold the circle at the top where the yarn crosses, and let the tail drop down at the back so that it falls across the centre of the loop. With your free hand or the tip of a crochet hook, pull a loop through the circle.

Holding the yarn

1 Pick up the yarn with your little finger in the opposite hand to your hook, with your palm facing upwards and with the short end in front. Turn your hand to face downwards, with the yarn on top of your index finger and under the other two fingers and wrapped right around the little finger, as shown above.

2 Turn your hand to face you, ready to hold the work in your middle finger and thumb. Keeping your index finger only at a slight curve, hold the work or the slip knot using the same hand, between your middle finger and your thumb and just below the crochet hook and loop/s on the hook.

2 Put the hook into the loop and pull gently so that it forms a loose loop on the hook.

Make a stitch

To create a stitch, catch the yarn from behind with the hook pointing upwards. As you gently pull the yarn through the loop on the hook, turn the hook so it faces downwards and slide the yarn through the loop. The loop on the hook should be kept loose enough for the hook to slide through easily.

Magic ring

This is a useful starting technique if you do not want a visible hole in the centre of your round. Loop the yarn around your finger, insert the hook through the ring, yarn round hook, and pull through the ring to make the first chain. Work the number of stitches required into the ring and then pull the end to tighten the centre ring.

Yarn round hook (yrh) & Chain (ch)

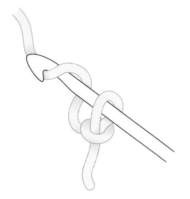 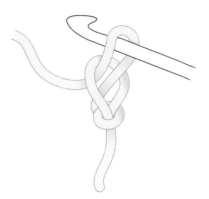

1 Using the hook, wrap the yarn round the hook (yrh) ready to pull it through the loop on the hook.

2 Pull through, creating a new loop on the hook (ch). Continue in this way to create a length of the required number of chains.

Making rows
When making straight rows you turn the work at the end of each row and make a turning chain to create the height you need for the stitch you are working with, as for Making rounds below.

Making rounds
When working in rounds the work is not turned, so you are always working from one side. Depending on the pattern you are working, a 'round' can be square. Start each round by making one or more chains to create the height you need for the stitch you are working:

Double crochet = 1 chain
Half treble crochet = 2 chain
Treble crochet = 3 chain

Work the required stitches to complete the round. At the end of the round, slip stitch into the top of the chain to close the round.

If you work in a spiral you do not need a turning chain.

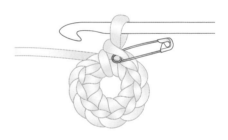

After completing your base ring, place a stitch marker in the first stitch and then continue to crochet around. When you have made a round and reached the point where the stitch marker is, work this stitch, take out the stitch marker from the previous round and put it back into the first stitch of the new round. A safety pin or piece of yarn in a contrasting colour is a good stitch marker.

Chain ring

If you are crocheting a round shape, one way of starting off is by crocheting a number of chains following the instructions in your pattern, and then joining them into a circle.

1 To join the chain into a circle, insert the crochet hook into the first chain that you made (not into the slip knot), yarn round hook.

2 Pull the yarn through the chain and through the loop on your hook at the same time, thereby creating a slip stitch and forming a circle. You now have a chain ring ready to work stitches into as instructed in the pattern.

Chain space (ch-sp)

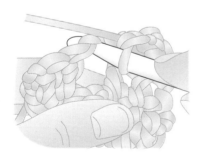

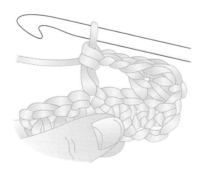

1 A chain space is the space that has been made under a chain in the previous round or row, and falls in between other stitches.

2 Stitches into a chain space are made directly into the hole created under the chain and not into the chain stitches themselves.

Working into top of stitch

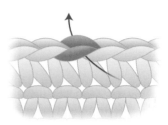

Unless otherwise directed, insert the hook under both of the two loops on top of the stitch – this is the standard technique.

Working into front loop of stitch (FLO)

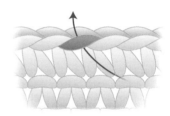

To work into the front loop of a stitch, pick up the front loop from underneath at the front of the work.

Working into back loop of stitch (BLO)

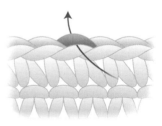

To work into the back loop of the stitch, insert the hook between the front and the back loop, picking up the back loop from the front of the work.

Slip stitch (sl st)

A slip stitch doesn't create any height and is often used as the last stitch to create a smooth and even round or row.

1 To make a slip stitch: first put the hook through the work, yarn round hook.

2 Pull the yarn through both the work and through the loop on the hook at the same time, so you will have one loop on the hook.

Double crochet (dc)

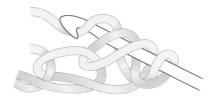

1 Insert the hook into your work, yarn round hook and pull the yarn through the work only. You will then have two loops on the hook.

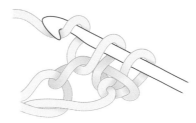

2 Yarn round hook again and pull through the two loops on the hook. You will then have one loop on the hook.

Joining new yarn

If using double crochet to join in a new yarn, insert the hook as normal into the stitch, using the original yarn, and pull a loop through. Drop the old yarn and pick up the new yarn. Wrap the new yarn round the hook and pull it through the two loops on the hook.

Half treble crochet (htr)

1 Before inserting the hook into the work, wrap the yarn round the hook and put the hook through the work with the yarn wrapped around.

2 Yarn round hook again and pull through the first loop on the hook. You now have three loops on the hook.

3 Yarn round hook and pull the yarn through all three loops. You will be left with one loop on the hook.

Treble crochet (tr)

1 Before inserting the hook into the work, wrap the yarn round the hook. Put the hook through the work with the yarn wrapped around, yarn round hook again and pull through the first loop on the hook. You now have three loops on the hook.

2 Yarn round hook again, pull the yarn through the first two loops on the hook. You now have two loops on the hook.

3 Yarn round hook, pull the yarn through two loops again. You will be left with one loop on the hook.

Double treble (dtr)

This stitch is longer than treble and requires more wraps of the yarn. It creates a very open fabric.

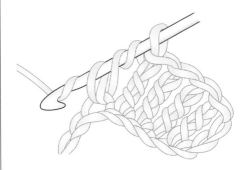

Yarn round hook twice, insert the hook in the stitch or chain, yarn round hook, pull the yarn through the work (4 loops on hook), (yarn round hook, pull yarn through first two loops on the hook) twice (2 loops on hook), yarn round hook, pull yarn through last two loops (1 loop on hook).

How to measure a tension square

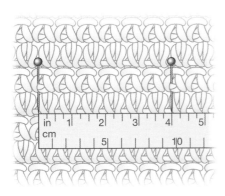

1 Using the hook and the yarn recommended in the pattern, make a number of chains to measure approximately 15cm (6in). Working in the stitch pattern given for the tension measurements, work enough rows to form a square. Fasten off.

2 Take a ruler, place it horizontally across the square, and using pins, mark a 10cm (4in) area. Repeat vertically to form a 10cm (4in) square on the fabric.

3 Count the number of stitches across, and the number of rows within

the square, and compare against the tension given in the pattern. If your numbers match the pattern then use this size hook and yarn for your project. If you have more stitches, then your tension is tighter than recommended and you need to use a larger hook. If you have fewer stitches, then your tension is looser and you will need a smaller hook.

4 Make tension squares using different size hooks until you have matched the tension in the pattern, and use this hook to make the project.

Front Post treble crochet (FPtr)

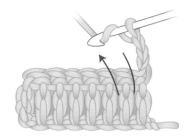

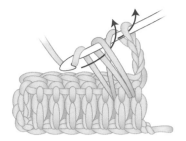

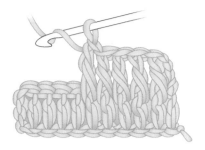

1 Yarn round hook and insert the hook from the front and around the post (the stem) of the next treble crochet from right to left.

2 Yarn round hook and pull the yarn through the work, yarn round hook and pull the yarn through the first 2 loops on the hook.

3 Yarn round hook and pull the yarn through the 2 loops on the hook (1 loop on hook). One Front Post treble completed.

Back Post treble crochet (BPtr)

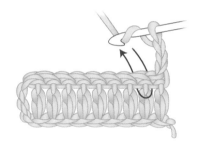

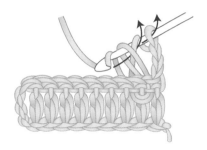

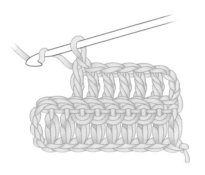

1 Yarn round hook and insert the hook from the back and around the post (the stem) of the next treble crochet as directed in the pattern from right to left.

2 Yarn round hook and pull the yarn through the work, yarn round hook and pull the yarn through the first 2 loops on the hook.

3 Yarn round hook and pull the yarn through the 2 loops on the hook (1 loop on hook). One Back Post treble crochet completed.

Changing colours/Joining at the end of a row or round

Note: You can use this technique when joining in a new ball of yarn as one runs out.

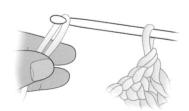

1 Keep the loop of the old yarn on the hook. Drop the tail and catch a loop of the strand of the new yarn with the crochet hook.

2 Pull the new yarn through the loop on the hook, keeping the old loop drawn tight and continue as instructed in the pattern.

Increasing

Make two or three stitches into one stitch or space from the previous row. The illustration shows a two-stitch treble crochet increase being made.

Decreasing

You can decrease by either missing the next stitch and continuing to crochet, or by crocheting two or more stitches together. The basic technique for crocheting stitches together is the same, no matter which stitch you are using. The following examples show dc2tog, htr2tog and tr2tog.

Double crochet two stitches together (dc2tog)

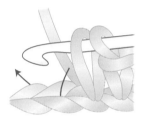

1 Insert the hook into your work, yarn round hook and pull the yarn through the work. You will then have two loops on the hook. Insert the hook in the next stitch, yarn round hook and pull the yarn through the work.

2 Yarn round hook again and pull through the three loops on the hook. You will then have one loop on the hook. One dc2tog made.

Half treble crochet two stitches together (htr2tog)

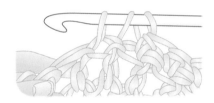

1 Yarn round hook, insert hook into next stitch, yarn round hook, draw yarn through. You now have three loops on the hook.

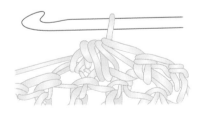

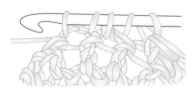

2 Yarn round hook, insert hook into next stitch, yarn round hook, draw yarn through. This leaves five loops on the hook.

3 Draw the yarn through all five loops on the hook. You will then have one loop on the hook. One htr2tog made.

Treble crochet two stitches together (tr2tog)

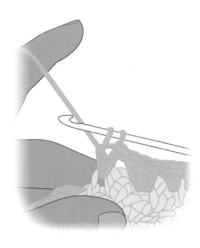

1 Yarn round hook, insert the hook into the next space, yarn round hook, pull the yarn through the work (3 loops on hook).

2 Yarn round hook, pull the yarn through two loops on the hook (2 loops on hook).

3 Yarn round hook, insert the hook into the next space.

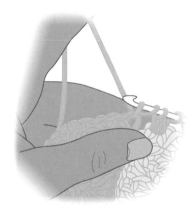

4 Yarn round hook, pull the yarn through the work (4 loops on hook).

5 Yarn round hook, pull the yarn through 2 loops on the hook (3 loops on hook).

6 Yarn round hook, pull the yarn through all 3 loops on the hook (1 loop on hook). One tr2tog made.

Sewing on a button

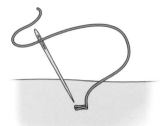

1 Mark the place where you want the button to go. Push the needle up from the back of the fabric and sew a few stitches over and over in this place.

2 Now bring the needle up through one of the holes in the button. Push the needle back down through the second hole and through the fabric. Bring it back up through the first hole. Repeat this five or six times. If there are four holes in the button, use all four of them to make a cross pattern. Make sure that you keep the stitches close together under the middle of the button.

Blocking

Crochet can tend to curl so to make flat pieces stay flat you may need to block them. Pin the piece out to the correct size and shape on the ironing board, then press or steam gently (depending on the type of yarn) and allow to dry completely.

Weaving in yarn ends

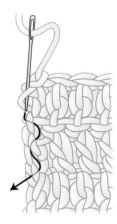

It is important to weave in the tail ends of the yarn so that they are secure and your crochet won't unravel. Thread a tapestry needle with the tail end of yarn. On the wrong side, take the needle through the crochet one stitch down on the edge, then take it through the stitches, working in a gentle zigzag. Work through 4 or 5 stitches then return in the opposite direction. Remove the needle, pull the crochet gently to stretch it, and trim the end.

Sewing up

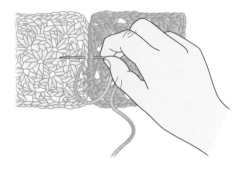

Sewing up crochet fabric can be done in many ways, but using a whip stitch is the easiest. However, you will be able to see the stitches clearly, so use a matching yarn. Lay the two pieces to be joined next to each other with right sides facing upwards. Secure the yarn to one piece. Insert the needle into the front of one piece of fabric, then up from the back of the adjoining fabric. Repeat along the seam.

CROCHET STITCH CONVERSION CHART

Crochet stitches are worked in the same way in both the UK and the USA, but the stitch names are not the same and identical names are used for different stitches. Below is a list of the UK terms used in this book, and the equivalent US terms.

UK TERM	US TERM
double crochet (dc)	single crochet (sc)
half treble crochet (htr)	half double crochet (hdc)
treble crochet (tr)	double crochet (dc)
double treble (dtr)	treble (tr)
tension	gauge
yarn round hook (yrh)	yarn over hook (yoh)

SUPPLIERS

UK

Yarn
Creative You
(for Hooplayarn and TekTek yarn)
www.creative-you.co.uk

Cygnet Yarns Limited
Tel: +44 (0) 1274 743374
www.cygnetyarns.com

Deramores
Tel: +44 (0)800 488 0708
www.deramores.com

Hobbycraft
Tel: +44 (0) 330 026 1400
www.hobbycraft.co.uk

John Lewis
Tel: +44 (0)3456 049049
www.johnlewis.com

Rowan
Tel: +44 (0)1484 681881
www.knitrowan.com
Sirdar
Tel: +44 (0)1924 231682
www.sirdar.co.uk

Wool and the Gang
www.woolandthegang.co.uk
Tel: +44 (0) 207 241 6420

Giant crochet hooks
Loop
Tel: +44 (0)20 7288 1160
www.loopknittingshop.com

Purlescence
Tel: +44 (0)1865 589944
www.purlescence.co.uk

USA AND CANADA

Yarn
Jones & Vandermeer
(for Hooplayarn)
Tel: +1-888-856-3820
www.jonesandvandermeer.com

Knitting Fever Inc.
www.knittingfever.com

Lion Brand Yarns
Tel: +1-800-258 YARN (9276)
www.lionbrand.com

Westminster Fibers
Tel: +1-800-445-9276
www.westminsterfibers.com

Yarnspirations.com
Tel: +1-888-368-8401
www.yarnspirations.com

Giant crochet hooks
The Bagsmith
Tel: +1-216-921-3535
www.bagsmith.com

Go-Girl Knitting
www.gogirlknitting.com

Loopy Mango
www.loopymango.com

General craft supplies
A.C. Moore
Tel: +1-888-226-6673
www.acmoore.com

Hobby Lobby
www.hobbylobby.com

Michaels
Tel: +1-800-642-4235
www.michaels.com

AUSTRALIA

Black Sheep Wool 'n' Wares
Tel: +61 (0)2 6779 1196
www.blacksheepwool.com.au

Creative Images Crafts
2141 Frankston-Flinders Road
Hastings VIC 3915
Tel: +61 (0)3 5979 1555

INTERNATIONAL

DMC
www.dmccreative.co.uk

Tjockt
www.tjockt.com

ACKNOWLEDGEMENTS

Firstly, I'd like to thank everyone at CICO for all their hard work, with a special shout out to Carmel and another to Fahema for all her lovely emails. More big thanks go to Rachel for her editing and Jemima for pattern checking – they taught me so much last time that hopefully this time wasn't so painful!

Particular thanks to Cygnet for prompt delivery and help with yarns, Cara at DMC for all her assistance with all sorts of yarns, Ingrid at Creative You for info and help with TekTek yarns and Hooplayarn for their generous offer.

I also have to thank my sister Katie – half of the projects in this book were suggested by her (mainly for her house, but still), Sarah Jay for the loan of a completely crazy knitting book, and a very, very big thank you to Kate Sully for all her help with inspiration and support. Last, but definitely not least, the amazing Neil Collins for making me such beautiful crochet hooks to begin with.

INDEX